D1783656

Teacher's Guide 2
Composition
Skills

Author: Chris Whitney

William Collins' dream of knowledge for all began with the publication of his first book in 1819.

A self-educated mill worker, he not only enriched millions of lives, but also founded a flourishing publishing house. Today, staying true to this spirit, Collins books are packed with inspiration, innovation and practical expertise. They place you at the centre of a world of possibility and give you exactly what you need to explore it.

Collins. Freedom to teach.

Published by Collins
An imprint of HarperCollins*Publishers*
The News Building
1 London Bridge Street
London
SE1 9GF

Browse the complete Collins catalogue at
www.collins.co.uk

© HarperCollins*Publishers* Limited 2017

10 9 8 7 6 5 4 3 2 1

ISBN 978-0-00-822303-8

British Library Cataloguing in Publication Data

A catalogue record for this publication is available from the British Library.

Publishing Director: Lee Newman
Publishing Manager: Helen Doran
Senior Editor: Hannah Dove
Project Manager: Emily Hooton
Author: Chris Whitney
Development Editors: Robert Anderson and Sarah Snashall
Copy-editor: Ros and Chris Davies
Proofreader: Tanya Solomons
Cover design and artwork: Amparo Barrera and Ken Vail Graphic Design
Internal design concept: Amparo Barrera
Typesetter: Jouve India Private Ltd
Illustrations: Alberto Saichann (Beehive Illustration)
Production Controller: Rachel Weaver

Printed and bound by CPI Group (UK) Ltd, Croydon, CR0 4YY

Acknowledgements

The publishers wish to thank the following for permission to reproduce content. Every effort has been made to trace copyright holders and to obtain their permission for the use of copyright materials. The publishers will gladly receive any information enabling them to rectify any error or omission at the first opportunity.

HarperCollins Publishers Ltd for an extract on page 41 from *The Stone Cutter* by Sean Taylor, copyright © 2005 Sean Taylor; for an extract on page 43 from *The Journey of the Humpback Whale* by Andy Belcher, copyright © 2012 HarperCollinsPublishers Ltd; for an extract on page 45 from *The Digestive System* by Harriet Blackford, © 2012 HarperCollinsPublishers Ltd; for an extract on page 47 from *Oliver* by Hilary McKay, copyright © 2012 Hilary McKay; for an extract on page 49 from *How to Make Pop-up Cards* by Monica Hughes, copyright © 2005 Monica Hughes; for an extract on page 54 from *Tig in the Dumps* by Michaela Morgan, copyright © 2005 Michaela Morgan; and for an extract on page 58 from *The Pot of Gold* by Julia Donaldson, copyright © 2006 Julia Donaldson. Reproduced by permission of HarperCollins Publishers Ltd.

Contents

About Treasure House

Treasure House is a comprehensive and flexible bank of books and online resources for teaching the English curriculum. The Treasure House series offers two different pathways: one covering each English strand discretely (Skills Focus Pathway) and one integrating texts and the strands to create a programme of study (Integrated English Pathway). This Teacher's Guide is part of the Skills Focus Pathway.

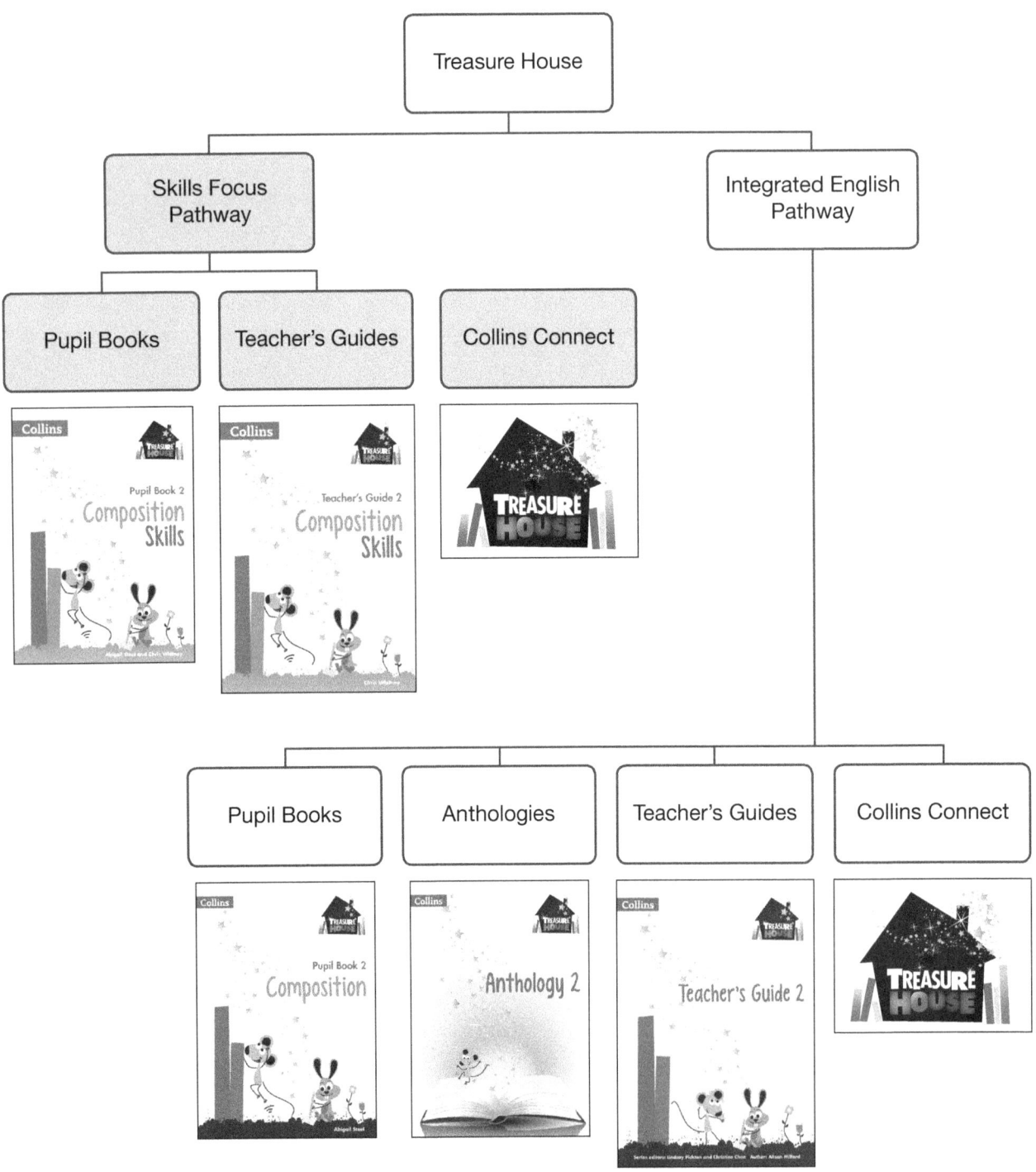

1. Skills Focus

The Skills Focus Pupil Books and Teacher's Guides for all four strands (Comprehension; Spelling; Composition; and Vocabulary, Grammar and Punctuation) allow you to teach each curriculum area in a targeted way. Each unit in the Pupil Book is mapped directly to the statutory requirements of the National Curriculum. Each Teacher's Guide provides step-by-step instructions to guide you through the Pupil Book activities and digital Collins Connect resources for each competency. With a clear focus on skills and clearly-listed curriculum objectives you can select the appropriate resources to support your lessons.

  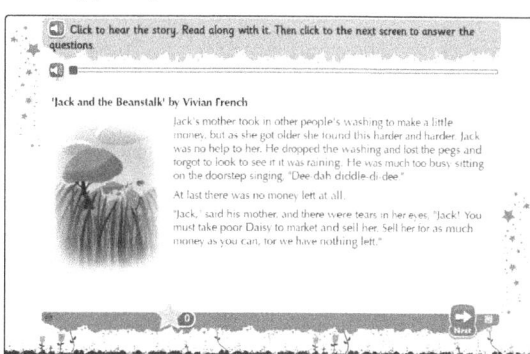

2. Integrated English

Alternatively, the Integrated English pathway offers a complete programme of genre-based teaching sequences. There is one Teacher's Guide and one Anthology for each year group. Each Teacher's Guide provides 15 teaching sequences focused on different genres of text such as fairy tales, letters and newspaper articles. The Anthologies contain the classic texts, fiction, non-fiction and poetry required for each sequence. Each sequence also weaves together all four dimensions of the National Curriculum for English – Comprehension; Spelling; Composition; and Vocabulary, Grammar and Punctuation – into a complete English programme. The Pupil Books and Collins Connect provide targeted explanation of key points and practice activities organised by strand. This programme provides 30 weeks of teaching inspiration.

   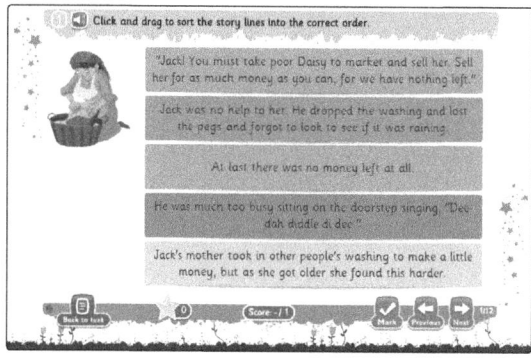

Other components

Handwriting Books, Handwriting Workbooks, Word Books and the online digital resources on Collins Connect are suitable for use with both pathways.

Treasure House Skills Focus Teacher's Guides

Year	Comprehension	Composition	Vocabulary, Grammar and Punctuation	Spelling
1	978-0-00-822290-1	978-0-00-822302-1	978-0-00-822296-3	978-0-00-822308-3
2	978-0-00-822291-8	978-0-00-822303-8	978-0-00-822297-0	978-0-00-822309-0
3	978-0-00-822292-5	978-0-00-822304-5	978-0-00-822298-7	978-0-00-822310-6
4	978-0-00-822293-2	978-0-00-822305-2	978-0-00-822299-4	978-0-00-822311-3
5	978-0-00-822294-9	978-0-00-822306-9	978-0-00-822300-7	978-0-00-822312-0
6	978-0-00-822295-6	978-0-00-822307-6	978-0-00-822301-4	978-0-00-822313-7

Inside the Skills Focus Teacher's Guides

The teaching notes in each unit in the Teacher's Guide provide you with subject information or background, a range of whole class and differentiated activities including photocopiable resource sheets and links to the Pupil Book and the online Collins Connect activities.

Each **Overview** provides clear objectives for each lesson tied into the new curriculum, links to the other relevant components and a list of any additional resources required.

Teaching overview provides a brief introduction to the specific skill concept or text type and some pointers on how to approach it.

Support, embed & challenge supports a mastery approach with activities provided at three levels.

Unit 18: Traditional tales (2)

Overview

English curriculum objectives
- **Reading:** Year 2 pupils should be taught to develop understanding of what they read by becoming increasingly familiar with and retelling a wider range of stories, fairy stories and traditional tales.
- **Writing:** Year 2 pupils should be taught to develop positive attitudes towards and stamina for writing by writing narratives about personal experiences and those of others (real and fictional).

Building towards
Children will plan and complete a story based on the theme of greed.

Treasure House resources
- Composition Skills Pupil Book 2, Unit 18, pages 49–51
- Photocopiable Unit 18, Resource 1: Story flowchart, page 105
- Photocopiable Unit 18, Resource 2: Gold, page 106

Additional resources
- A selection of books and websites including traditional tales for children to browse and read

Introduction

Teaching overview
In this unit children learn about traditional tales and write their own middle and end to a story starter. This unit focuses on some of the stock elements of a traditional tale (moral theme, a sudden visitor, asking for kindness).

Introduce the concept
Ask: 'Do you know of any stories where people argue a lot, especially over money?' Explain that this story is about two people who argue and who meet a mysterious little man.

Then ask: 'Have you read stories about hidden treasure?' Recount some to the group. Discuss if it is always lucky to discover treasure. Ask: 'Are there any stories where it is unlucky in the end to have found the treasure?'

Read the extract together. Ask: 'Do you think that Sandy and Bonny are going to end up rich by the end of the story? What else might happen?' Discuss different options. Explain that often in traditional tales greedy people do not usually end up rich! (Though kind people often do.) Ask: 'Do you think that the little man really needs somewhere to stay the night?' Discuss the traditional elements of sudden wealth, siblings, little people testing us, and so on.

Pupil practice

Get started
The children add the missing words to the sentences using the text as reference.

Answers
1. Sandy and Bonny kept <u>sheep</u>.   [1 mark]
2. The two of them were always <u>arguing</u>.   [1 mark]
3. One evening, they were busy arguing when there was a <u>tap at the door</u>.   [1 mark]
4. There on the doorstep stood a <u>little man</u>. [1 mark]
5. He wore a <u>green hat</u> and a <u>ragged green coat</u>.   [2 marks]

Try these
Children answer the questions to give them an overview of the story, before suggesting the next events in the story, based on their understanding so far (and their understanding of traditional stories).

Pupil Book pages 49–51

Answers
1. Because he took out two gold coins   [1 mark]
2. greedy   [1 mark]
3. gold coins/gold/treasure   [1 mark]
4. Accept any appropriate answer.   [1 mark]

Now try these
Children build on their ideas in **Try these** to write the middle and the ending of this traditional tale based on greed. Their sentences should begin where the text ends with Sandy spotting something gleaming. You may wish to use the activities and photocopiables in **Support** and **Embed** to give differentiated support with these activities.

Support, embed & challenge

Support
Unit 18 Resource 1: Story flowchart provides structure in the form of a flowchart for the children to use to compose the end of their story using the process suggested in **Now try these**. Explain that each circle should cover one event.

Embed
Ask the children to use the storyboard provided (Unit 18 Resource 2: Gold) to plan the ending to the traditional tale (**Now try these**), adding accompanying sentences on the writing frame.

Challenge
Ask the children to write a new tale based on the theme of greed.

Homework / Additional activities

Greedy!
Ask the children to research other tales that contain a greedy character. They might think of fairy stories or other traditional tales they have read or seen on screen. They should then choose one of the characters, describe them and explain why they think they act as they do. Do they get what they deserved or not?

Introduce the concept/text provides 5–10 minutes of preliminary discussion points or class/group activities to get the pupils engaged in the lesson focus and set out any essential prior learning.

Pupil practice gives guidance and the answers to each of the three sections in the Pupil Book: *Get started*, *Try these* and *Now try these*.

Homework / Additional activities lists ideas for classroom or homework activities, and relevant activities from Collins Connect.

Two photocopiable **resource** worksheets per unit provide differentiated support for the writing task in each lesson. They are designed to be used with the activities in support or embed sections.

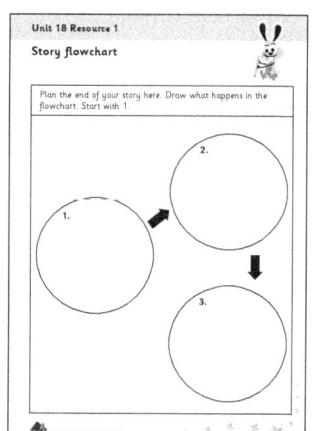

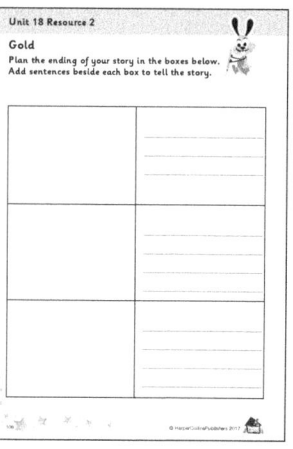

Treasure House Skills Focus Pupil Books

There are four Skills Focus Pupil Books for each year group, based on the four dimensions of the National Curriculum for English: Comprehension; Spelling; Composition; and Vocabulary, Grammar and Punctuation. The Pupil Books provide a child-friendly introduction to each subject and a range of initial activities for independent pupil-led learning. A Review unit for each term assesses pupils' progress.

Year	Comprehension	Composition	Vocabulary, Grammar and Punctuation	Spelling
1	978-0-00-823634-2	978-0-00-823646-5	978-0-00-823640-3	978-0-00-823652-6
2	978-0-00-823635-9	978-0-00-823647-2	978-0-00-823641-0	978-0-00-823653-3
3	978-0-00-823636-6	978-0-00-823648-9	978-0-00-823642-7	978-0-00-823654-0
4	978-0-00-823637-3	978-0-00-823649-6	978-0-00-823643-4	978-0-00-823655-7
5	978-0-00-823638-0	978-0-00-823650-2	978-0-00-823644-1	978-0-00-823656-4
6	978-0-00-823639-7	978-0-00-823651-9	978-0-00-823645-8	978-0-00-823657-1

Inside the Skills Focus Pupil Books

Comprehension

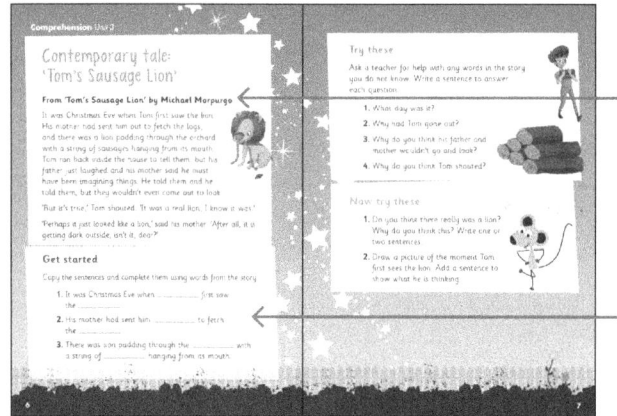

Includes high-quality text extracts covering poetry, prose, traditional tales, playscripts and non-fiction.

Pupils retrieve and record information, learn to draw inferences from texts and increase their familiarity with a wide range of literary genres.

Composition

Includes high-quality, annotated text extracts as models for different types of writing.

Children learn how to write effectively and for a purpose.

Vocabulary, Grammar and Punctuation

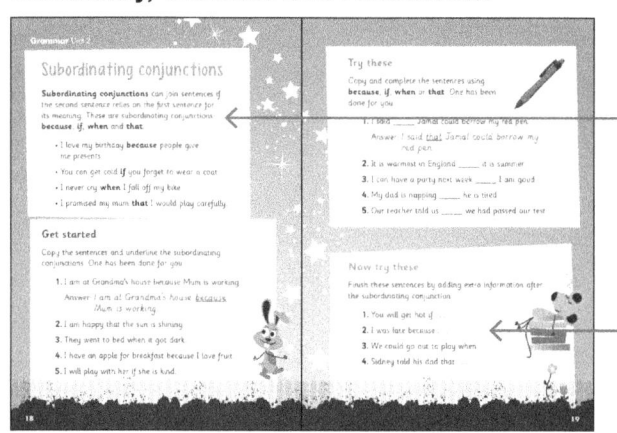

Develops children's knowledge and understanding of grammar and punctuation skills.

A rule is introduced and explained. Children are given lots of opportunities to practise using it.

Spelling

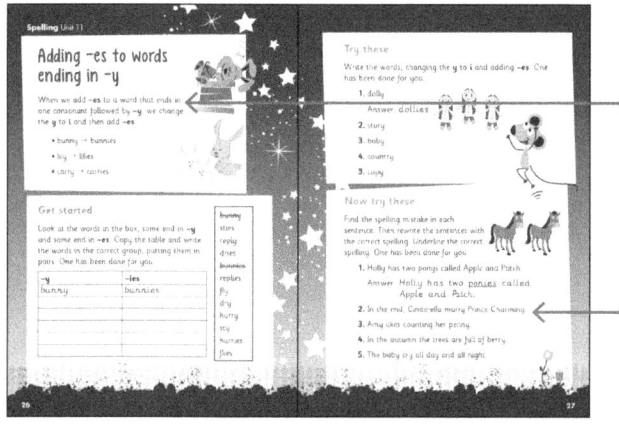

Spelling rules are introduced and explained.

Practice is provided for spotting and using the spelling rules, correcting misspelt words and using the words in context.

Treasure House on Collins Connect

Digital resources for Treasure House are available on Collins Connect which provides a wealth of interactive activities. Treasure House is organised into six core areas on Collins Connect:

- Comprehension
- Spelling
- Composition
- Vocabulary, Grammar and Punctuation
- The Reading Attic
- Teacher's Guides and Anthologies.

For most units in the Skills Focus Pupil Books, there is an accompanying Collins Connect unit focused on the same teaching objective. These fun, independent activities can be used for initial pupil-led learning, or for further practice using a different learning environment. Either way, with Collins Connect, you have a wealth of questions to help children embed their learning.

Treasure House on Collins Connect is available via subscription at connect.collins.co.uk

Features of Treasure House on Collins Connect

The digital resources enhance children's comprehension, spelling, composition, and vocabulary, grammar, punctuation skills through providing:

- a bank of varied and engaging interactive activities so children can practise their skills independently
- audio support to help children access the texts and activities
- auto-mark functionality so children receive instant feedback and have the opportunity to repeat tasks.

Teachers benefit from useful resources and time-saving tools including:

- teacher-facing materials such as audio and explanations for front-of-class teaching or pupil-led learning
- lesson starter videos for some Composition units
- downloadable teaching notes for all online activities
- downloadable teaching notes for Skills Focus and Integrated English pathways
- the option to assign homework activities to your classes
- class records to monitor progress.

Comprehension

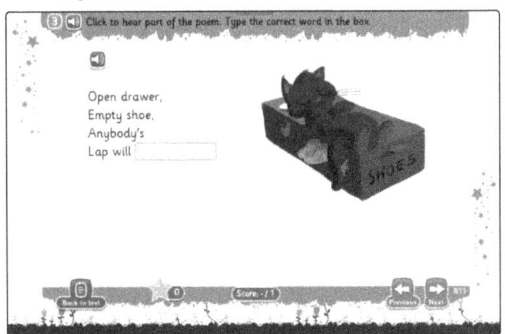

- Includes high-quality text extracts covering poetry, prose, traditional tales, playscripts and non-fiction.
- Audio function supports children to access the text and the activities

Composition

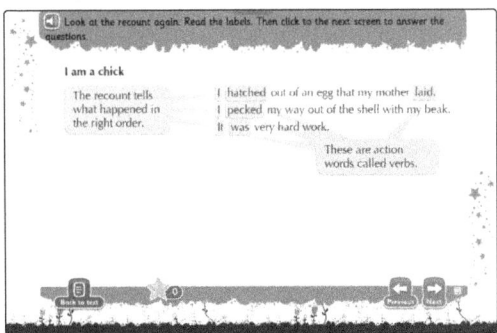

- Activities support children to develop and build more sophisticated sentence structures.
- Every unit ends with a longer piece of writing that can be submitted to the teacher for marking.

Vocabulary, Grammar and Punctuation

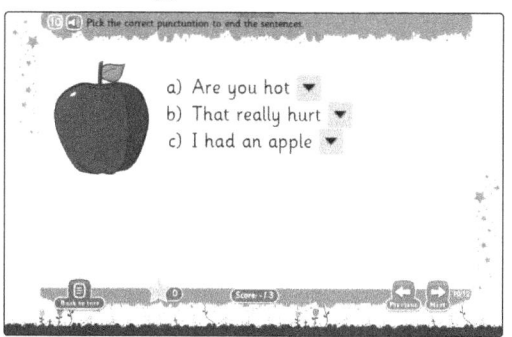

- Fun, practical activities develop children's knowledge and understanding of grammar and punctuation skills.
- Each skill is reinforced with a huge, varied bank of practice questions.

Spelling

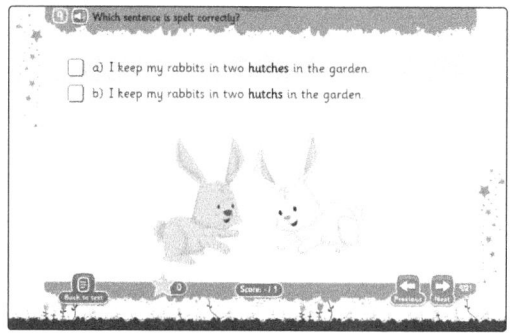

- Fun, practical activities develop children's knowledge and understanding of each spelling rule.
- Each rule is reinforced with a huge, varied bank of practice questions.
- Children spell words using an audio prompt, write their own sentences and practise spelling using Look Say Cover Write Check.

Reading Attic

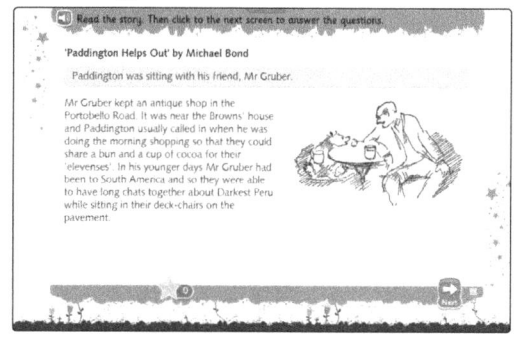

- Children's love of reading is nurtured with texts from exciting children's authors including Michael Bond, David Walliams and Michael Morpurgo.
- Lesson sequences accompany the texts, with drama opportunities and creative strategies for engaging children with key themes, characters and plots.
- Whole-book projects encourage reading for pleasure.

Treasure House Digital Teacher's Guides and Anthologies

The teaching sequences and anthology texts for each year group are included as a flexible bank of resources.

The teaching notes for each skill strand and year group are also included on Collins Connect.

Support, embed and challenge

Treasure House provides comprehensive, detailed differentiation at three levels to ensure that all children are able to access achievement. It is important that children master the basic skills before they go further in their learning. Children may make progress towards the standard at different speeds, with some not reaching it until the very end of the year.

In the Teacher's Guide, Support, Embed and Challenge sections allow teachers to keep the whole class focussed with no child left behind. Two photocopiable resources per unit offer additional material linked to the Support, Embed or Challenge sections.

Support

The Support section offers simpler or more scaffolded activities that will help learners who have not yet grasped specific concepts covered. Background information may also be provided to help children to contextualise learning. This enables children to make progress so that they can keep up with the class.

To help with children's composition skills, activities are broken down into smaller steps, for example, children draw pictures, write plans or complete templates before writing sentences.

If you have a teaching assistant, you may wish to ask him or her to help children work through these activities. You might then ask children who have completed these activities to progress to other more challenging tasks found in the Embed or Challenge sections – or you may decide more practice of the basics is required. Collins Connect can provide further activities.

Embed

The Embed section includes activities to embed learning and is aimed at those who children who are working at the expected standard. It ensures that learners have understood key teaching objectives for the age-group. These activities could be used by the whole class or groups, and most are appropriate for both teacher-led and independent work.

In Composition, children can practise their writing skills using templates, plans and prompts allowing them to write a variety of text-types at the required standard.

Challenge

The Challenge section provides additional tasks, questions or activities that will push children who have mastered the concept without difficulty. This keeps children motivated and allows them to gain a greater depth of understanding. You may wish to give these activities to fast finishers to work through independently.

In Composition, children's writing skills can be enhanced with the freer activities in the Challenge section, for example, they may write an alternative ending to a story, retell a story in their own words or think about a story from another perspective. Children can demonstrate more advanced use of vocabulary and manipulate grammar more accurately through these tasks.

Assessment

Teacher's Guide

There are opportunities for assessment throughout the Treasure House series. The teaching notes in Treasure House Teacher's Guides offer ideas for questions, informal assessment and spelling tests.

Pupil Book Review units

Each Pupil Book has three Review units designed as a quick formative assessment tool for the end of each term. Questions assess the work that has been covered over the previous units. These review units will provide you with an informal way of measuring your pupils' progress. You may wish to use these as Assessment for Learning to help you and your pupils to understand where they are in their learning journey.

In Treasure House, there is a strong focus on genres of texts that widen children's knowledge of writing for different purposes and audiences. In Composition, the review units allow children to demonstrate what they know in independent tasks. Vocabulary, grammar and punctuation can be assessed through their writing as well as their understanding of a genre.

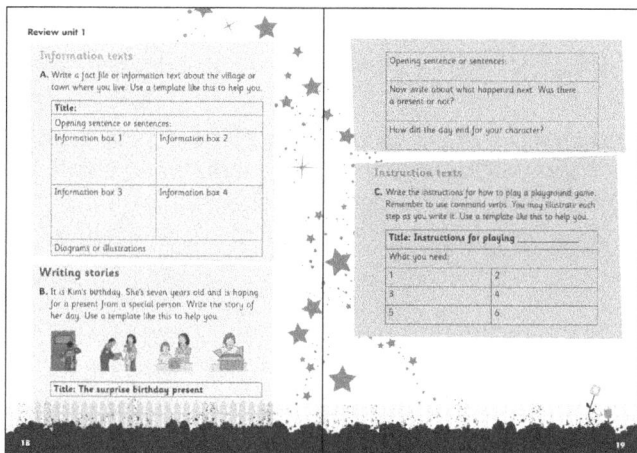

Assessment in Collins Connect

Activities on Collins Connect can also be used for effective assessment. Activities with auto-marking mean that if children answer incorrectly, they can make another attempt helping them to analyse their own work for mistakes. Homework activities can also be assigned to classes through Collins Connect. At the end of activities, children can select a smiley face to indicate how they found the task giving you useful feedback on any gaps in knowledge.

Class records on Collins Connect allow you to get an overview of children's progress with several features. You can choose to view records by unit, pupil or strand. By viewing detailed scores, you can view pupils' scores question by question in a clear table-format to help you establish areas where there might be particular strengths and weaknesses both class-wide and for individuals.

If you wish, you can also set mastery judgements (mastery achieved and exceeded, mastery achieved, mastery not yet achieved) to help see where your children need more help.

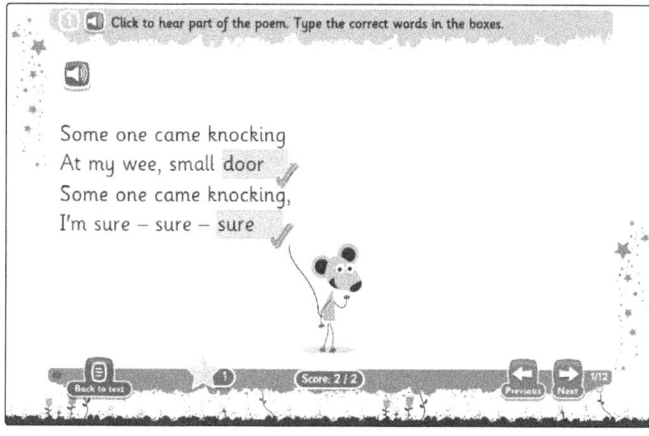

Support with teaching composition

Composition is one of the four core dimensions of the National Curriculum for English. Within the teaching of English, the aim is to ensure that all pupils write clearly, accurately and coherently, adapting their language and style in and for a range of contexts, purposes and audiences.

Effective composition involves forming, articulating and communicating ideas, and then organising them coherently for a reader. This requires clarity and an awareness of the audience, purpose and context. All children can be helped towards better writing if shown how to generate and organise ideas appropriately and how to then transfer them successfully from plan to page. In addition, pupils need to be taught how to plan, revise and evaluate their writing. These aspects of writing have been incorporated into the Treasure House Composition Skills strand.

Throughout the primary years, we want pupils to have opportunities to write for a range of real purposes and audiences as part of their work across the curriculum. These purposes and audiences should underpin the decisions about the form the writing should take, such as a narrative, an explanation or a description. We want pupils to develop positive attitudes towards their writing and stamina for it by writing narratives about personal experiences and those of others, by writing about real events, by writing poetry and by writing for different purposes.

Pupils also need to be taught to monitor whether their own writing makes sense. They should also understand, through being shown, the skills and processes essential for writing: the generation of ideas, initial drafting, and re-reading to check that the meaning is clear.

Treasure House Composition Skills Teacher's Guides provide extensive notes and guidance for teaching a range of genres and text types. The integrated pupil books provide opportunities for pupils to plan, draft and edit their writing. Each unit is linked to an extract of quality text from which the teaching ideas are taken.

GLOSSARY	
Word	Definition

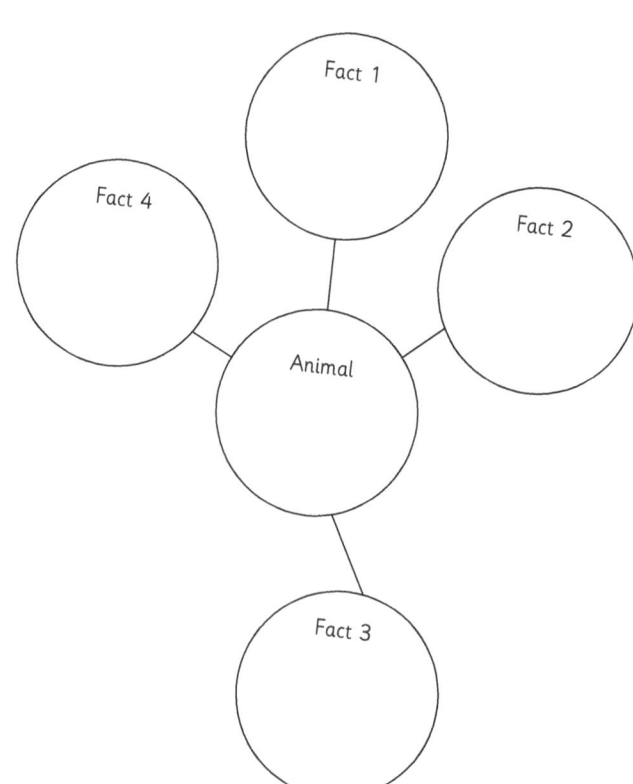

Delivering the 2014 National Curriculum for English

Unit	Title	Treasure House Resources	Collins Connect	English Programme of Study

1	Personal stories (1)	• Composition Skills Pupil Book 2, Unit 1, pages 4–5
		• Composition Skills Teacher's Guide 2
		  – Unit 1, pages 22–23
		  – Photocopiable Unit 1, Resource 1: What does Brown Bear do next? page 65
		  – Photocopiable Unit 1, Resource 2: What happens next? page 66
			Collins Connect Treasure House Composition Year 2, Unit 1	**Reading:** Becoming increasingly familiar with and retelling a wider range of stories, fairy stories and traditional tales
				Writing: Writing narratives about personal experiences and those of others (real and fictional)

2	Fairy tales	• Composition Skills Pupil Book 2, Unit 2, pages 6–7
		• Composition Skills Teacher's Guide 2
		  – Unit 2, pages 24–25
		  – Photocopiable Unit 2, Resource 1: My story map, page 67
		  – Photocopiable Unit 2, Resource 2: Fairy tale ending, page 68
			Collins Connect Treasure House Composition Year 2, Unit 2	**Reading:** Becoming increasingly familiar with and retelling a wider range of stories, fairy stories and traditional tales.
				Writing: Writing narratives about personal experiences and those of others (real and fictional).

3	Traditional tales (1)	• Composition Skills Pupil Book 2, Unit 3, pages 8–9
		• Composition Skills Teacher's Guide 2
		  – Unit 3, pages 26–27
		  – Photocopiable Unit 3, Resource 1: Hungry animals, page 69
		  – Photocopiable Unit 3, Resource 2: Animal thieves, page 70
			Collins Connect Treasure House Composition Year 2, Unit 3	**Reading:** Becoming increasingly familiar with and retelling a wider range of stories, fairy stories and traditional tales.
				Writing: Writing narratives about personal experiences and those of others (real and fictional).

Unit	Title	Treasure House Resources	Collins Connect	English Programme of Study

4	Information writing	• Composition Skills Pupil Book 2, Unit 4, pages 10–11
		• Composition Skills Teacher's Guide 2
		  – Unit 4, pages 28–29
		  – Photocopiable Unit 4, Resource 1: My school, page 71
		  – Photocopiable Unit 4, Resource 2: School report, page 72
			Collins Connect Treasure House Composition Year 2, Unit 4	**Reading:** Being introduced to non-fiction books that are structured in different ways.
				Writing: Writing for different purposes.

5	Reports	• Composition Skills Pupil Book 2, Unit 5, pages 12–13
		• Composition Skills Teacher's Guide 2
		  – Unit 5, pages 30–31
		  – Photocopiable Unit 5, Resource 1: Report template, page 73
		  – Photocopiable Unit 5, Resource 2: My report, page 74
			Collins Connect Treasure House Composition Year 2, Unit 5	**Reading:** Being introduced to non-fiction books that are structured in different ways.
				Writing: Writing for different purposes.

6	Simple instructions	• Composition Skills Pupil Book 2, Unit 6, pages 14–15
		• Composition Skills Teacher's Guide 2
		  – Unit 6, pages 32–33
		  – Photocopiable Unit 6, Resource 1: How to …, page 75
		  – Photocopiable Unit 6, Resource 2: Keep the classroom tidy, page 76
			Collins Connect Treasure House Composition Year 2, Unit 6	**Reading:** Being introduced to non-fiction books that are structured in different ways.
				Writing: Writing for different purposes.

7	Simple explanations	• Composition Skills Pupil Book 2, Unit 7, pages 16–17
		• Composition Skills Teacher's Guide 2
		  – Unit 7, pages 34–35
		  – Photocopiable Unit 7, Resource 1: Riding a bicycle, page 77
		  – Photocopiable Unit 7, Resource 2: How bicycles move, page 78
			Collins Connect Treasure House Composition Year 2, Unit 7	**Reading:** Being introduced to non-fiction books that are structured in different ways.
				Writing: Writing for different purposes.

Unit	Title	Treasure House Resources	Collins Connect	English Programme of Study

8	Poetry: Wordplay	• Composition Skills Pupil Book 2, Unit 8, pages 20–21
		• Composition Skills Teacher's Guide 2
		  – Unit 8, pages 37–38
		  – Photocopiable Unit 8, Resource 1: My toys, page 82
		  – Photocopiable Unit 8, Resource 2: Toy poem, page 83
			Collins Connect Treasure House Composition Year 2, Unit 8	**Reading:** Listening to, discussing and expressing views about a wide range of contemporary and classic poetry.
				Writing: Writing poetry.

9	Poetry: Alligator	• Composition Skills Pupil Book 2, Unit 9, pages 22–24
		• Composition Skills Teacher's Guide 2
		  – Unit 9, pages 39–40
		  – Photocopiable Unit 9, Resource 1: Animal poetry, page 84
		  – Photocopiable Unit 9, Resource 2: Insulting animals poem, page 85
			Collins Connect Treasure House Composition Year 2, Unit 9	**Reading:** Listening to, discussing and expressing views about a wide range of contemporary and classic poetry.
				Writing: Writing poetry.

10	Stories from another culture	• Composition Skills Pupil Book 2, Unit 10, pages 25–26
		• Composition Skills Teacher's Guide 2
		  – Unit 10, pages 41–42
		  – Photocopiable Unit 10, Resource 1: The Stone Cutter's story, page 86
		  – Photocopiable Unit 10, Resource 2: What happened next? page 87
				Reading: Becoming increasingly familiar with and retelling a wider range of stories, fairy stories and traditional tales.
				Writing: Writing narratives about personal experiences and those of others (real and fictional).

11	Information writing: Fact files	• Composition Skills Pupil Book 2, Unit 11, pages 27–29
		• Composition Skills Teacher's Guide 2
		  – Unit 11, pages 43–44
		  – Photocopiable Unit 11, Resource 1: Animal facts, page 88
		  – Photocopiable Unit 11, Resource 2: Animal vocabulary, page 89
				Reading: Being introduced to non-fiction books that are structured in different ways.
				Writing: Writing for different purposes.

Unit	Title	Treasure House Resources	Collins Connect	English Programme of Study

12	Explanation writing: Healthy eating	• Composition Skills Pupil Book 2, Unit 12, pages 30–32
		• Composition Skills Teacher's Guide 2
		  – Unit 12, pages 45–46
		  – Photocopiable Unit 12, Resource 1: Healthy eating, page 90
		  – Photocopiable Unit 12, Resource 2: A healthy lunch, page 91
				Reading: Being introduced to non-fiction books that are structured in different ways.
				Writing: Writing for different purposes.

13	Stories set long ago	• Composition Skills Pupil Book 2, Unit 13, pages 33–35
		• Composition Skills Teacher's Guide 2
		  – Unit 13, pages 47–48
		  – Photocopiable Unit 13, Resource 1: Gruel for dinner, page 92
		  – Photocopiable Unit 13, Resource 2: What happened to Oliver? page 93
				Reading: Becoming increasingly familiar with and retelling a wider range of stories, fairy stories and traditional tales.
				Writing: Writing narratives about personal experiences and those of others (real and fictional).

14	Instructions	• Composition Skills Pupil Book 2, Unit 14, pages 36–37
		• Composition Skills Teacher's Guide 2
		  – Unit 14, pages 49–50
		  – Photocopiable Unit 14, Resource 1: Fruit salad, page 94
		  – Photocopiable Unit 14, Resource 2: Game instructions, page 95
				Reading: Being introduced to non-fiction books that are structured in different ways.
				Writing: Writing for different purposes.

15	Poetry: Animal rhymes	• Composition Skills Pupil Book 2, Unit 15, pages 40–42
		• Composition Skills Teacher's Guide 2
		  – Unit 15, pages 52–53
		  – Photocopiable Unit 15, Resource 1: Frog poem, page 99
		  – Photocopiable Unit 15, Resource 2: Three verses, page 100
				Reading: Listening to, discussing and expressing views about a wide range of contemporary and classic poetry.
				Writing: Writing poetry.

Unit	Title	Treasure House Resources	Collins Connect	English Programme of Study
16	Narrative	• Composition Skills Pupil Book 2, Unit 16, pages 43–45 • Composition Skills Teacher's Guide 2 – Unit 16, pages 54–55 – Photocopiable Unit 16, Resource 1: Tig's story, page 101 – Photocopiable Unit 16, Resource 2: What happens to Tig? page 102		**Reading:** Becoming increasingly familiar with and retelling a wider range of stories, fairy stories and traditional tales. **Writing:** Writing narratives about personal experiences and those of others (real and fictional).
17	Non-chronological report	• Composition Skills Pupil Book 2, Unit 17, pages 46–48 • Composition Skills Teacher's Guide 2 – Unit 17, pages 56–57 – Photocopiable Unit 17, Resource 1: Animal key facts, page 103 – Photocopiable Unit 17, Resource 2: Animal report, page 104		**Reading:** Being introduced to non-fiction books that are structured in different ways. **Writing:** Writing for different purposes.
18	Traditional tales (2)	• Composition Skills Pupil Book 2, Unit 18, pages 49–51 • Composition Skills Teacher's Guide 2 – Unit 18, pages 58–59 – Photocopiable Unit 18, Resource 1: Story flowchart, page 105 – Photocopiable Unit 18, Resource 2: Gold, page 106		**Reading:** Becoming increasingly familiar with and retelling a wider range of stories, fairy stories and traditional tales. **Writing:** Writing narratives about personal experiences and those of others (real and fictional).

Unit	Title	Treasure House Resources	Collins Connect	English Programme of Study
19	Myths	• Composition Skills Pupil Book 2, Unit 19, pages 52–54 • Composition Skills Teacher's Guide 2 – Unit 19, pages 60–61 – Photocopiable Unit 19, Resource 1: Daedalus and Icarus's escape, page 107 – Photocopiable Unit 19, Resource 2: What do Daedalus and Icarus do next? page 108		**Reading:** Becoming increasingly familiar with and retelling a wider range of stories. **Writing:** Writing narratives about personal experiences and those of others (real and fictional).
20	Personal stories (2)	• Composition Skills Pupil Book 2, Unit 20, pages 55–56 • Composition Skills Teacher's Guide 2 – Unit 20, pages 62–63 – Photocopiable Unit 20, Resource 1: My story mountain, page 109 – Photocopiable Unit 20, Resource 2: My storyboard, page 110		**Reading:** Becoming increasingly familiar with and retelling a wider range of stories, fairy stories and traditional tales. **Writing:** Writing narratives about personal experiences and those of others (real and fictional).

Unit	Title	Treasure House Resources	Collins Connect	English Programme of Study
	All units			The following statutory requirements can be covered throughout the programme:
				Pupils should be taught to:
				• develop positive attitudes towards and stamina for writing by:
				– writing about real events
				• consider what they are going to write before beginning by:
				– planning or saying out loud what they are going to write about
				– writing down ideas and/or key words, including new vocabulary
				– encapsulating what they want to say, sentence by sentence
				• make simple additions, revisions and corrections to their own writing by:
				– evaluating their writing with the teacher and other pupils
				– re-reading to check that their writing makes sense and that verbs are used correctly and consistently, including verbs in the continuous form
				– proof-reading to check for errors in spelling, grammar and punctuation [for example, ends of sentences punctuated correctly]
				• read aloud what they have written with appropriate intonation to make the meaning clear.

Unit 1: Personal stories (1)

Overview

English curriculum objectives

- **Reading:** Year 2 pupils should be taught to develop understanding of what they read by becoming increasingly familiar with and retelling a wider range of stories, fairy stories and traditional tales.
- **Writing:** Year 2 pupils should be taught to develop positive attitudes towards and stamina for writing by writing narratives about personal experiences and those of others (real and fictional).

Building towards

Children will plan and write their own continuation of a narrative.

Treasure House resources

- Composition Skills Pupil Book 2, Unit 1, pages 4–5
- Collins Connect Treasure House Composition Year 2, Unit 1
- Photocopiable Unit 1, Resource 1: What does Brown Bear do next? page 65
- Photocopiable Unit 1, Resource 2: What happens next? page 66

Additional resources

- Other stories where something or someone is lost, for example *Lost and Found* by Oliver Jeffers and/or the film of this book

Introduction

Teaching overview

In this unit children learn about writing stories, using their own experiences or those of others.

The unit focuses on reading and completing a story based on a personal feeling of loss, attempting to understand and then capture the main character's feelings. It provides opportunities to discuss the theme of loss and to complete a story about a bear who loses his sense of smell. Children can be challenged at the end to write their own story about losing something or being lost.

Introduce the concept

Ask the children to share if they have ever lost anything. Ask: 'What happened?', 'Was it found?'

Discuss with the children any stories or films they know about something or someone being lost. They might know the book and film *Lost and Found* by Oliver Jeffers. Read the story opening on Pupil Book page 4. Ask: 'What is Brown Bear's problem? How can he hunt without his sense of smell?'

Pupil practice

Pupil Book pages 4–5

Get started

The children draw and label pictures of the things that Brown Bear remembers smelling.

Try these

Children complete sentences to show an understanding of the story. Ask the children to picture Brown Bear walking through the forest and imagine how he is feeling before completing the sentences. Accept appropriate answers.

Now try these

The children to carry out activities 1 and 2 to help them understand and engage with the situation at the end of the extract. Next, ask the children to discuss activity 3 with a partner, sharing different ideas before planning and writing the end of the story. The story should show Brown Bear's sadness at his loss and then go on to describe what happens next, bringing the story to a resolution. Finally, in activity 4, ask those children who will benefit from a challenge to plan a new story on the theme of loss. Remind the children that it does not have to be about a bear – it could be about another animal or a small child. Accept correctly demarcated sentences.

You may wish to use the activities and photocopiables in **Support** and **Embed** to give differentiated support with these activities.

Support, embed & challenge

Support

Unit 1 Resource 1: What does Brown Bear do next? provides a storyboard template for children who need additional support to use to draw four key events to complete the story. Encourage the children to use the two boxes for **Now try these** activities 1 and 2, and the second two boxes to finish the story. When they have finished, ask the children to use their storyboard to tell their story ending to their partner.

Embed

Tell the children to use Unit 1 Resource 2: What happens next? to capture their ideas for the rest of the story, using the first two boxes for **Now try these** activities 1 and 2 and the last two boxes to complete the story, writing a caption for each picture. Ask them to use their completed storyboard to tell their story ending to a partner, using and expanding the sentences they wrote.

Challenge

Ask these children to write their own story on the theme of 'lost'; it may be personal or inspired by a story or film.

Homework / Additional activities

Getting lost

Ask the children to write a few sentences about a time when they or a friend were lost. They have been talking and writing about losing something but now they consider if they or a friend have ever been lost.

Collins Connect: Unit 1

Ask the children to complete Unit 1 (see Teach → Year 2 → Composition → Unit 1).

Unit 2: Fairy tales

Overview

English curriculum objectives

- **Reading:** Year 2 pupils should be taught to develop understanding of what they read by becoming increasingly familiar with and retelling a wider range of stories, fairy stories and traditional tales.
- **Writing:** Year 2 pupils should be taught to develop positive attitudes towards and stamina for writing by writing narratives about personal experiences and those of others (real and fictional).

Building towards

Children will plan and write their own story about the main character.

Treasure House resources

- Composition Skills Pupil Book 2, Unit 2, pages 6–7
- Collins Connect Treasure House Composition Year 2, Unit 2
- Photocopiable Unit 2, Resource 1: My story map, page 67
- Photocopiable Unit 2, Resource 2: Fairy tale ending, page 68

Additional resources

- Film clip showing the character Puss in Boots
- Books or websites that include the fairy tale 'Puss in Boots'

Introduction

Teaching overview

In this unit children read, listen to and retell the classic fairy tale 'Puss in Boots'.

The unit focuses on developing an understanding of the characters in the fairy tale. It provides opportunities to discuss these characters and why they act as they do. After writing their version of the end of the fairy tale, the children are challenged to consider a new story for the main character.

Introduce the concept

Watch a clip from a film showing the character of Puss in Boots.

Discuss the differences between a pet cat and the Puss in Boots character in the fairy tale. What do the children think this tells us about fairy tales?

Ask the children to tell you what they know about Puss in Boots. If they are not familiar with the story, tell a simple version of the story to them (ensuring that the version you tell fits with the activities in the Pupil Book). Afterwards, work together to create a pictorial story map of the tale on the board.

Read the story opener on Pupil Book page 6 together.

Pupil practice

Get started

The children add the missing words from the fairy tale to the spaces in the sentences.

Answers

1. Once upon a time, there was a <u>windmill</u> on top of a hill. [1 mark]
2. In the <u>windmill</u> there lived an <u>old</u> <u>man</u> and his three sons. [2 marks]
3. The eldest son was given the <u>windmill</u>. [1 mark]
4. The second son was given a <u>donkey</u>. [1 mark]
5. The youngest son was given a <u>cat</u>. [1 mark]

Try these

Children complete the sentences to create the rest of the story, working in pairs remembering the fairy tale together. Leave the story map from the starter on the board to support the children. Accept any ideas that are appropriate.

Now try these

Children will use their imaginations to create their own story that continues from the opener on Pupil Book page 6. Ask the children to carry out activities 1, 2 and 3 to create the characters of the boy and Puss. Tell them to plan, rehearse, then storyboard with speech bubbles or write their new tale.

You may wish to use the activities and photocopiables in **Support** and **Embed** to give differentiated support with these activities.

Support, embed & challenge

Support

Reread the story opener on Pupil Book page 6 to these children and ask them carry out **Now try these** activities 1 to 3. When they are ready to move onto activity 4, ask them to discuss in pairs what might happen next. Encourage the children to change the story, but celebrate any attempts at storytelling, even if it remains close to the original. Tell them to capture their story in five pictures using Unit 2 Resource 1: My story map. Ask them to write a speech bubble for two of the pictures. Encourage them to tell their story to a partner.

Embed

Ask the children to draw a storyboard (Unit 2 Resource 2: Fairy tale ending) using their ideas for how the story continues (**Now try these** activity 4) and ends, and consider the words they will use as they tell it.

Challenge

Using books or the internet, these children should research the fairy tale 'Puss in Boots' and retell the story in their own words.

Homework / Additional activities

Magical cats

Ask the children to write their own fairy story about a magical cat.

Collins Connect: Unit 2

Ask the children to complete Unit 2 (see Teach → Year 2 → Composition → Unit 2).

Unit 3: Traditional tales (1)

Overview

English curriculum objectives

- **Reading:** Year 2 pupils should be taught to develop understanding of what they read by becoming increasingly familiar with and retelling a wider range of stories, fairy stories and traditional tales.
- **Writing:** Year 2 pupils should be taught to develop positive attitudes towards and stamina for writing by writing narratives about personal experiences and those of others (real and fictional).

Building towards

Children will plan and write their own animal fable.

Treasure House resources

- Composition Skills Pupil Book 2, Unit 3, pages 8–9
- Collins Connect Treasure House Composition Year 2, Unit 3
- Photocopiable Unit 3, Resource 1: Hungry animals, page 69
- Photocopiable Unit 3, Resource 2: Animal thieves, page 70

Additional resources

- Books and websites containing more fables, including Aesop's

Introduction

Teaching overview

In this unit children learn about traditional tales and fables and write their own version.

The unit focuses on understanding the main character in the tale and the reasons for his/her actions. It provides opportunities to discuss fables and the moral lessons they teach.

Introduce the concept

Ask: 'Have you have ever heard of Aesop's fables?' Read a short fable to them and discuss how a fable always has a moral. This may need some explanation.

Explain that this extract comes from one of Aesop's fables and is only part of the story. Read the extract together.

Ask: 'Do you know what a crow is?', 'Have you seen one in a garden or park?'

Pupil practice

Pupil Book pages 8–9

Get started

The children add the missing words to the sentences, using their own ideas. Check that the words are appropriate.

Try these

Children answer the questions then use their answers to create their own (verbal if appropriate) story opening for 'The Fox and the Crow'. Accept any ideas that are appropriate to the tale. They should use the illustration at the top of page 8 for ideas.

Now try these

The children use activities 1, 2 and 3 to continue their own version of 'The Fox and the Crow'. Ask the children to consider the genre (fable), the title and the crow's behaviour when deciding how to continue the story.

Activity 4: Children use their knowledge of fables to write another story about an animal that takes some food. It might be helpful here to read the original fable in its entirety if this has not been done before. It may provide them with ideas.

You may wish to use the activities and photocopiables in **Support** and **Embed** to give differentiated support with these activities.

Support, embed & challenge

Support

Share a version of the full story of 'The Fox and the Crow' with these children. Allow them to focus on retelling this fable rather than creating their own version for **Now try these** activities 1, 2 and 3. When moving on to activity 4, Unit 3 Resource 1: Hungry animals provides structure for those needing additional support to tell their story.

Embed

Ask the children to use Unit 3 Resource 2: Animal thieves to create a storyboard for their new story (**Now try these** activity 4) and consider the words they will use as they tell it.

Challenge

Ask the children to find more Aesop's fables on the internet. Ask them to learn one and tell it to the rest of the class, explaining why they like it.

Homework / Additional activities

Traditional tale

Ask the children to write a short summary of another traditional tale that they like.

Collins Connect: Unit 3

Ask the children to complete Unit 3 (see Teach → Year 2 → Composition → Unit 3).

Unit 4: Information writing

Overview

English curriculum objectives

- Reading: Year 2 pupils should be taught to develop understanding of what they read by being introduced to non-fiction books that are structured in different ways.
- Writing: Year 2 pupils should be taught to write for different purposes.

Building towards

Children will write an information text about their school with a labelled diagram.

Treasure House resources

- Composition Skills Pupil Book 2, Unit 4, pages 10–11
- Collins Connect Treasure House Composition Year 2, Unit 4
- Photocopiable Unit 4, Resource 1: My school, page 71
- Photocopiable Unit 4, Resource 2: School report, page 72

Additional resources

- Non-fiction books and websites about natural disasters such as volcanoes and earthquakes
- Film clips of a volcano erupting and about Pompeii

Introduction

Teaching overview

In this unit children learn to write information texts.

The unit focuses on how information texts are characterised by facts, and stresses the difference between fact and opinion.

Introduce the concept

Show a short film clip of a volcano erupting.

Ask: 'Have you heard about a famous volcano in Italy called Vesuvius?' Tell them about it if not and about the eruption in ancient Roman times. Source a film clip about Pompeii suitable for children.

Tell the children that we can learn about things and events in information texts. Discuss what kinds of things they might see in an information text: text with lots of accurate facts (not opinions); pictures; diagrams and captions. Read the extract together. Point out the features: past tense, facts, specific vocabulary.

Pupil practice

Pupil Book pages 10–11

Get started

In this activity the children decide if a sentence contains fact or opinion.

Answers

1. fact		[1 mark]
2. opinion		[1 mark]
3. opinion		[1 mark]
4. fact		[1 mark]
5. fact		[1 mark]

Try these

Children retrieve facts from the text as they answer the questions.

Answers

1. Vesuvius erupting		[1 mark]
2. It began to erupt in AD 79.		[1 mark]
3. A mighty earthquake shook the ground.		[1 mark]
4. The eruption lasted for two days.		[1 mark]
5. 9		[1 mark]

Now try these

First, the children use the information in text to create a labelled picture of Vesuvius, then imagine the effect of the explosion on those watching it. Next the children write their own information text about their school.

1. Ideas for words children could include on their labels: clouds of ash, massive explosion, rocks, red-hot lava, clouds of burning gas, falling ash, black 'snow'

2. Accept children's drawings showing the people of Pompeii watching Vesuvius erupt.

3. Children complete the picture with speech bubbles showing what the people are saying.

4. They plan their idea for an information text about their school. They include a labelled illustration and some written sentences.

You may wish to use the activities and photocopiables in **Support** and **Embed** to give differentiated support with these activities.

Support, embed & challenge

Support

Ask the children to complete the information text about their school (**Now try these** activity 4) using the structured support (Unit 4 Resource 1: My school). Sentences have been constructed and children have to add the missing information. When they have finished, ask the children to tell you which statements in their text are fact and which are opinions. Remind them that information texts will be mainly facts.

Embed

Ask the children to complete an information text about their school (**Now try these** activity 4) using the template provided (Unit 4 Resource 2: School report). Remind the children that their information text must start with facts, even if it moves on to include opinions.

Challenge

Ask the children to write an information text about their village or town. They may make notes prior to writing and include labelled pictures of notable places.

Homework / Additional activities

Visitor guide

Ask the children to write an information text about a place they have visited on holiday. They could start this by writing some questions that a visitor might need the answer to.

Collins Connect: Unit 4

Ask the children to complete Unit 4 (see Teach → Year 2 → Composition → Unit 4).

Unit 5: Reports

Overview

English curriculum objectives

- **Reading:** Year 2 pupils should be taught to develop understanding of what they read by being introduced to non-fiction books that are structured in different ways.
- **Writing:** Year 2 pupils should be taught to write for different purposes.

Building towards

Children will write a non-chronological report about a subject they have been studying at school. This could be part of their topic work across the curriculum.

Treasure House resources

- Composition Skills Pupil Book 2, Unit 5, pages 12–13
- Collins Connect Treasure House Composition Year 2, Unit 5
- Photocopiable Unit 5, Resource 1: Report template, page 73
- Photocopiable Unit 5, Resource 2: My report, page 74

Additional resources

- Non-fiction books about the Ancient Egyptians
- Short documentary about the Ancient Egyptians
- Books and websites relating to the class topic

Introduction

Teaching overview

In this unit children learn to write a non-chronological report. The unit focuses on the structure of a report.

Introduce the concept

Ask: 'Do you know any facts about Egypt?', 'Has anyone been there?', Where is it on a map?'

Ask: 'What do you know about the people who lived there thousands of years ago?'

If possible, watch a short documentary and discuss how the information is presented.

Discuss with children what they know about writing a non-chronological report. Ensure that children know this type of report summarises facts about the subject in clearly organised sections and uses technical vocabulary. Read the report together and help the children to locate the features discussed.

Pupil practice

Pupil Book pages 12–13

Get started

In this activity the children decide which information is 'true' and which is 'false'.

Answers

1. true   [1 mark]
2. true   [1 mark]
3. false   [1 mark]
4. false   [1 mark]
5. false   [1 mark]

Try these

Children retrieve the facts from the text and consider the different sections of the report.

Answers

1. Ancient Egyptians   [1 mark]
2. Ancient Egyptians / Pharaohs and pyramids   [1 mark]
3. Farmers who lived along the banks of the Nile   [1 mark]
4. Pharaohs and pyramids   [1 mark]
5. Accept any three facts from the passage. [1 mark]

Now try these

Activities 1, 2 and 3: To further understand the features of a non-chronological report, the children use the information to draw a labelled diagram of a pyramid, then suggest an additional section and a word bank. Activity 4: Children will complete this section by planning and writing a non-chronological report linked to one area of the Year 2 curriculum. Accept relevant research questions/key words from children. Children may use the photocopiables for support with this text type.

You may wish to use the activities and photocopiables in **Support** and **Embed** to give differentiated support with these activities.

Support, embed & challenge

Support

Unit 5 Resource 1: Report template provides a simple template to which children can add key facts about their chosen subject for **Now try these** activity 4. When this is completed, they could write sentences about their topic in their books adding a labelled diagram and a word bank if possible.

Embed

Ask the children to remember the features of a report that they read about and used in this unit so far (subheadings, facts, labelled diagrams, word bank, and so on). Ask the children to use Unit 5 Resource 2: My report as a framework for their non-chronological report (**Now try these** activity 4).

Challenge

Ask the children to choose their own subject matter to write a report about. It could be based on their hobbies or interests. Encourage them to use subheadings, a word bank and an illustration.

Homework / Additional activities

Hobbies and interests

Ask the children to write a short report about the hobbies or interests of a member of their family. They should set it out as they have learned in this unit.

Collins Connect: Unit 5

Ask the children to complete Unit 5 (see Teach → Year 2 → Composition → Unit 5).

Unit 6: Simple instructions

Overview

English curriculum objectives

- **Reading:** Year 2 pupils should be taught to develop understanding of what they read by being introduced to non-fiction books that are structured in different ways.
- **Writing:** Year 2 pupils should be taught to write for different purposes.

Building towards

Children will write their own set of instructions, choosing from a given list

Treasure House resources

- Composition Skills Pupil Book 2, Unit 6, pages 14–15
- Collins Connect Treasure House Composition Year 2, Unit 6
- Photocopiable Unit 6, Resource 1: How to ..., page 75
- Photocopiable Unit 6, Resource 2: Keep the classroom tidy, page 76

Additional resources

- Instructions for how to use household objects such as a microwave and/or a recipe book
- A TV clip where a presenter makes something

Introduction

Teaching overview

In this unit children learn to write a set of instructions.

The unit focuses on understanding the features of an instruction text, including the use of imperative verbs, using a statement of purpose, diagrams and sequential order.

Introduce the concept

Show a set of instructions for using a household object or making a recipe and explain how they should be followed. Discuss what makes this easier. Read together the extract and ask the children to locate: imperative (command) verbs, sequential

language and logical order. Together, write an introductory statement of purpose that could be used at the beginning. Discuss the use of numbered points in some instructions. Ask the children, in pairs, to decide where they could put numbers in this set of instructions.

Discuss with the children what instructions they have followed recently.

Watch a children's TV programme where an item is made and discuss the process. As you watch, ask the children to listen out for the logical order of the instructions, sequential language and command words.

Pupil practice

Pupil Book pages 14–15

Get started

Children first read the text as a model. Then children use any suitable imperative (command) verbs to complete the sentences. Other answers are possible.

Answers

1. <u>Find</u> the things you will need. [1 mark]
2. <u>Wash</u> your hands. [1 mark]
3. <u>Put/place</u> the items on the table. [1 mark]
4. <u>Read</u> the instructions carefully. [1 mark]
5. <u>Clean</u> the table afterwards. [1 mark]

Try these

Children write one part, for example the first line, of the instructions for each given task. Accept relevant answers with a command verb. Afterwards, share the children's answers and model adding sequential language to the beginning of each.

Now try these

Activity 1: Children answer the question about instruction writing. Activities 2 and 3: children draw and label two different diagrams in order to practise using useful diagrams in instruction texts. Encourage them to use the illustration on Pupil Book page 15 for support. Activity 4: the children write their own instructions, choosing from a given list. Check for accurate sequencing and imperative (command) verbs.

Answer

1. imperative

You may wish to use the activities and photocopiables in **Support** and **Embed** to give differentiated support with these activities.

Support, embed & challenge

Support

Unit 6 Resource 1: How to … provides a template for those needing additional support with **Now try these** activity 4. It provides children with the opportunity to write the instructions and draw a diagram alongside these.

Embed

After the children have carried out the activities in the Pupil Book, ask them to write a list of instructions for how to keep their classroom tidy. Unit 6 Resource 2: Keep the classroom tidy provides a template for additional practice.

Challenge

Ask the children to write a clear set of instructions for how to organise a birthday party or directions for how to get from their home to the school.

Homework / Additional activities

How to …

Ask the children to write a set of instructions for something that needs to be done at home. This could be 'Instructions for getting ready for school'.

Collins Connect: Unit 6

Ask the children to complete Unit 6 (see Teach → Year 2 → Composition → Unit 6).

Unit 7: Simple explanations

Overview

English curriculum objectives

- **Reading:** Year 2 pupils should be taught to develop understanding of what they read by being introduced to non-fiction books that are structured in different ways.
- **Writing:** Year 2 pupils should be taught to write for different purposes.

Building towards

Children will write a short explanation text.

Treasure House resources

- Composition Skills Pupil Book 2, Unit 7, pages 16–17
- Collins Connect Treasure House Composition Year 2, Unit 7

- Photocopiable Unit 7, Resource 1: Riding a bicycle, page 77
- Photocopiable Unit 7, Resource 2: How bicycles move, page 78

Additional resources

- Film clip of a kite flying
- A selection of non-fiction books that explain how things work for children to browse and refer to
- Examples of imaginary machines such as the ones in *Charlie and the Chocolate Factory* by Roald Dahl and the series of animations 'Wallace and Gromit's Cracking Contraptions'

Introduction

Teaching overview

In this unit children learn to write explanations.

The unit focuses on understanding what an explanation text is. Children read an example text and then write a short explanation of their own.

Introduce the concept

Show a short film clip of a kite flying in the sky. Ask: 'Has anyone ever flown a kite?' Then ask:

'Do you know how a kite works?' Together, read the explanation on Pupil Book page 16 on how to fly a kite. Point out the present tense verbs and the precise vocabulary. Discuss the difference between an instruction and an explanation.

Discuss with the children what an 'explanation' is. Ask them to explain how a pencil sharpener works. Make sure children are not giving instructions but are explaining the mechanical process.

Pupil practice

Pupil Book pages 16–17

Get started

The children read the extract then decide whether a sentence is 'true' or 'false'.

Answers

1. false		[1 mark]
2. false		[1 mark]
3. true		[1 mark]
4. false		[1 mark]
5. true		[1 mark]

Try these

Children complete the sentences using their knowledge of kite flying. Afterwards, share the answers and discuss how the answers provide specific and useful information about kites.

Possible answers

1. A kite is a <u>frame covered in light material.</u> [1 mark]

2. It is best to fly a kite when <u>it is windy.</u> [1 mark]

3. If you are in a busy park, <u>be careful of the string getting tangled.</u> [1 mark]

4. Your string might <u>get tangled or might break.</u> [1 mark]

5. Flying a kite is <u>an exciting thing to do.</u> [1 mark]

Now try these

Children answer questions using explanatory sentences. They may need reminding that verbs are used in the present tense in explanations. Ask the children to use the introductory extract as a model for their explanation texts.

You may wish to use the activities and photocopiables in **Support** and **Embed** to give differentiated support with these activities.

Support, embed & challenge

Support

Reread the extract with the children, pointing out the features of an explanation text: present tense, illustrations, clear explanations. Unit 7 Resource 1: Riding a bicycle provides a template for those needing additional support to complete the **Now try these** activity 4.

Embed

Ask the children to use Unit 7 Resource 2: How bicycles move (flowchart) to structure a simple explanation text showing the stages of the process of riding a bicycle. (**Now try these** activity 4). Afterwards, ask the children to use their flow chart, talking about each picture. Encourage them to use language such as 'first' and 'then'.

Challenge

Ask the children to write a further simple explanation of how something works, for example the lunch system at school. Their explanation should include a flowchart or labelled diagram.

Homework / Additional activities

My imaginary machine

Show and talk about some imaginary machines in books and films. Ask the children to invent a machine of their choice. What can it do and how does it do it? They should draw a flowchart or labelled diagram to accompany their explanation.

Collins Connect: Unit 7

Ask the children to complete Unit 7 (see Teach → Year 2 → Composition → Unit 7).

Review unit 1

These tasks provide the children with the opportunity to apply and demonstrate the skills they have learned. Explain to the children that they now have an opportunity to show their skills independently.

A. Information texts

Read the task through with the children and make sure they have understood what to do. You may wish to give Review unit 1 Resource 1: My town, page 79 to children to use as a template.

Look for evidence of children's developing understanding of and writing of information texts. Significant features to look out for include:

- the use of subheadings to structure the information into sections
- present tense
- technical language
- possible diagrams or illustrations.

B. Writing stories

Read the task through with the children and make sure they have understood what to do. You may wish to give children Review unit 1 Resource 2: Kim's birthday, page 80 to use as a template.

Look for evidence of children's developing understanding of and writing of narrative. Significant features to look out for include:

- past tense
- the use of time language (adverbials) to structure events – after that, later on and so on
- correctly demarcated sentences
- noun phrases
- conjunctions linking sentences.

C. Instruction texts

Read the task through with the children and make sure they have understood what to do. You may wish to give children Review unit 1 Resource 3: How to play a game, page 81 to complete the activity.

Look for evidence of children's developing understanding of and writing of instruction texts. Significant features to look out for include:

- imperative (command) verbs
- sequential language
- logical order of instructions
- possible use of diagrams
- possible statement of purpose at the beginning and statement at the end.

Unit 8: Poetry: Wordplay

Overview

English curriculum objectives

- **Reading:** Year 2 pupils should be taught to listen to, discuss and express views about a wide range of contemporary and classic poetry.
- **Writing:** Year 2 pupils should be taught to develop positive attitudes towards and stamina for writing by writing poetry.

Building towards

Children will write their own poem using wordplay.

Treasure House resources

- Composition Skills Pupil Book 2, Unit 8, pages 20–21
- Collins Connect Treasure House Composition Year 2, Unit 8

- Photocopiable Unit 8, Resource 1: My toys, page 82
- Photocopiable Unit 8, Resource 2: Toy poem, page 83

Additional resources

- A range of poetry books and websites with poems emphasising wordplay for children to browse and read

Introduction

Teaching overview

In this unit children learn to write a poem using wordplay.

The unit focuses on wordplay, showing how when writing poetry we can be much freer in our use of language than in narrative, even making up new words and phrases if we want.

Introduce the concept

Use the text in the Pupil Book to discuss with children how poetry differs from 'normal' writing (for example when telling a story). Explore issues such as rhyme and rhythm and then move on to the words themselves.

Ask: 'What do you notice about the words used in this poem?' Encourage the children to notice that many are made up and even a bit 'silly'. The poet is having fun!

You might like to share some more poems with wordplay at the end of the lesson or encourage children to share ones they themselves have found.

Pupil practice

Pupil Book pages 20–21

Get started

In this activity the children are asked to decide if the sentences are true or false. Ask the children to reread the poem in pairs before answering the questions.

Answers

1. true		[1 mark]
2. true		[1 mark]
3. true		[1 mark]
4. true		[1 mark]
5. false		[1 mark]

Try these

Children add the most appropriate words or phrases (discuss how they may be hyphenated) to the sentences. Take feedback and discuss.

Now try these

1 and 2: The children respond to the poem by describing Sluggery-wuggery and then deciding what they would say to him. 3. The children write two nonsense lines starting 'My age is ...' 4. Children write their own poem about a different subject (their toys), using the model presented in the poem by Pauline Clarke.

You may wish to use the activities and photocopiables in **Support** and **Embed** to give differentiated support with activity 4.

Support, embed & challenge

Support

Unit 8 Resource 1: My toys provides a template for children needing additional support with **Now try these** activity 4. They choose their toys and draw a picture of them. They then add a 'silly' phrase describing them. One example is given.

Embed

Ask the children to write a poem about their toys (as suggested in **Now try these** activity 4) using Sluggery-wuggery by Pauline Clarke as a model.

Unit 8 Resource 2: Toy poem provides a simple template. Children could continue by choosing to write in the same style about another topic – for example, 'My friend is …'

Challenge

Ask the children to write their own poem in the style of the poem by Pauline Clarke. They choose the content and attempt a rhyme. They should concentrate on wordplay, including making up their own silly words.

Homework / Additional activities

My funny family poem

Ask the children to choose a member of their family to write a poem about. They should use the style shown in this unit and start by thinking of some funny words and phrases to describe the person.

Collins Connect: Unit 8

Ask the children to complete Unit 8 (see Teach → Year 2 → Composition → Unit 8).

Unit 9: Poetry: Alligator

Overview

English curriculum objectives

- **Reading:** Year 2 pupils should be taught to listen to, discuss and express views about a wide range of contemporary and classic poetry.
- **Writing:** Year 2 pupils should be taught to develop positive attitudes towards and stamina for writing by writing poetry.

Building towards

Children will write a list poem about an animal of their choice using the model provided and by choosing appropriate vocabulary.

Treasure House resources

- Composition Skills Pupil Book 2, Unit 9, pages 22–24

- Collins Connect Treasure House Composition Year 2, Unit 9
- Photocopiable Unit 9, Resource 1: Animal poetry, page 84
- Photocopiable Unit 9, Resource 2: Insulting animals poem, page 85

Additional resources

- Non-fiction books and websites about wild and/or dangerous animals
- Film clips showing alligators and other animals in action – to help children choose the most appropriate vocabulary

Introduction

Teaching overview

In this unit children learn to write a list poem with descriptive words.

This unit focuses on the words to describe an animal and then listing them. The text extract is a humorous poem.

Introduce the concept

Ask: 'Do you know what an alligator is?', 'Have any of you ever seen an alligator in real life?', 'Do you know any stories about alligators?'

Show a short film clip of alligators and ask children to describe their features.

Discuss how this list of descriptive sentences can be used as the basis of a poem. Read the poem on Pupil Book page 22 together. Read and enjoy each 'insult' and discuss what it is describing. Ask the children on their opinion of the poet's logic. Unpick the use of 'dem'.

Pupil practice

Pupil Book pages 22–24

Get started

In this activity the children are asked to decide if the sentences are true or false. Ask the children to reread the poem before completing the activity.

Answers

1. false		[1 mark]
2. true		[1 mark]
3. false		[1 mark]
4. true		[1 mark]
5. false		[1 mark]

Try these

Children add the most appropriate animal to the description. Challenge the children to make up lines for a cat, a bear and a shark.

Possible answers

1. call <u>frog</u> wide-mouth		[1 mark]
2. call <u>hamster</u> short-legs		[1 mark]
3. call <u>tiger</u> razor-claws		[1 mark]
4. call <u>elephant</u> wobble-nose		[1 mark]
5. call <u>dog</u> messy-paws		[1 mark]

Now try these

Activities 1, 2 and 3: The children engage with the poem by drawing a picture and labelling it, deciding what the alligator would say back and finally writing two positive names for the alligator. Activity 4: Children write their own poem about a different animal using the model presented in the text extract.

Answers

1. Accept drawings that show the main features of the alligator.
2. The alligator's words should be added in a speech bubble.
3. Children may need help with the word 'insulting'.

4. Accept poems about other animals with some attempt to use the model provided.

You may wish to use the activities and photocopiables in **Support** and **Embed** to give differentiated support with activity 4.

Support, embed & challenge

Support

Unit 9 Resource 1: Animal poetry provides a template of the poem for children needing additional support for **Now try these** activity 4. They should choose their animal and think of the words they could use to 'insult' or call the creature. They can add pictures to their poem.

Embed

Show children some more clips of wild or dangerous animals to help them to choose a dangerous animal to write their poem (**Now try these** activity 4) about, using the extract as a model. Unit 9 Resource 2: Insulting animals poem provides a simple template on which the children can write their poem.

Challenge

Ask the children to choose a dangerous animal to write their poem about. They should consider why the creature is dangerous and think about what the poem's last two lines will be (see the last two lines in the John Agard poem). Their aim is to create the same type of humour. They can then complete the writing of the poem as before.

Homework / Additional activities

My animal poem

Ask the children to find other poems written about animals. They should read a few and then attempt to use one as a model to write a poem about an animal of their choice or even their pet. They could suggest 'insult' names to call it!

Collins Connect: Unit 9

Ask the children to complete Unit 9 (see Teach → Year 2 → Composition → Unit 9).

Unit 10: Stories from another culture

Overview

English curriculum objectives

- **Reading:** Year 2 pupils should be taught to develop understanding by becoming increasingly familiar with and retelling a wider range of stories, fairy stories and traditional tales.
- **Writing:** Year 2 pupils should be taught to develop positive attitudes towards and stamina for writing by writing narratives about personal experiences and those of others (real and fictional).

Building towards

Children will continue and close a traditional story, considering the theme of the story.

Treasure House resources

- Composition Skills Pupil Book 2, Unit 10, pages 25–26
- Photocopiable Unit 10, Resource 1: The Stone Cutter's story, page 86
- Photocopiable Unit 10, Resource 2: What happened next? page 87

Additional resources

- Other stories from another culture with a related or other strong theme for children to browse and read

Introduction

Teaching overview

In this unit children learn to write the ending of a story based on a theme.

The unit focuses on understanding the theme in a traditional tale from another country – in this case, Japan. It provides opportunities to discuss familiar story themes and for children to link themes to their own experience.

Introduce the concept

Ask: 'Have you ever been unhappy with something you have, wishing it were something else, or that you had something different?'

Discuss with the children whether they think bigger and better things always make people happy. Suggest that this is the 'theme' of the story they are about to read. You may need to explore the idea of the theme of a story, discussing how this is different from the plot or narrative.

Ask: 'Do you know where Japan is?' Show Japan on a map or interactive whiteboard. Explain the role of a stone cutter.

Read the extract, explaining that it is only the opening section of the story. Discuss what the theme – or main idea – might be. Perhaps 'always wanting more' or 'being unhappy with who we are'.

Pupil practice

Pupil Book pages 25–26

Get started

Ask the children to reread the story. The children add the missing words from the given text to the spaces in the sentences.

Answers

1. First of all the poor stone cutter wanted to be a <u>rich</u> <u>man</u>. [1 mark]
2. Then he wanted to be an <u>emperor</u>. [1 mark]
3. The emperor was dressed in <u>blue</u> and <u>gold</u>. [1 mark]
4. The sun was more <u>powerful</u> than any emperor. [1 mark]

Try these

Children answer the questions to create the rest of the story.

Answers

1. He was poor. [1 mark]
2. rich [1 mark]
3. the sun [1 mark]
4. Accept answers that say he will never be happy. Some children might add that he will not be happy because he has not found happiness in the other things he wanted to be. [1 mark]

Now try these

Children should use their prediction skills to write further sentences for the story. The activities support the children as they build up and end the story. Tell the children to remember the theme and the dissatisfied character of the stone cutter as they write. Tell them to decide what should happen to the stone cutter at the end.

You may wish to use the activities and photocopiables in **Support** and **Embed** to give differentiated support with the activities in **Now try these**.

Support, embed & challenge

Support

Before the children carry out the activities in **Now try these**, ask them to use the storyboard on Unit 10 Resource 1: The Stone Cutter's story to plan their ideas for how the story of the stone cutter continues and ends.

Embed

Ask the children to use Unit 10 Resource 2: What happened next? to capture their answers to **Now try these** and illustrate them. Remind them to keep in mind the theme of the story, to add three different new elements and an ending that fits with the story.

Challenge

Ask the children to write another story with a similar theme. It could be based on a character who is never happy with what they have.

Homework / Additional activities

Stories from afar

Ask the children to research stories that come from other countries and to write a short summary of one such story. What do they think the theme of their chosen story is?

Unit 11: Information writing: Fact files

Overview

English curriculum objectives

- **Reading:** Year 2 pupils should be taught to develop understanding of what they read by being introduced to non-fiction books that are structured in different ways.
- **Writing:** Year 2 pupils should be taught to write for different purposes.

Building towards

Children will write an information text (fact file) about an animal of their choice showing understanding of the text features.

Treasure House resources

- Composition Skills Pupil Book 2, Unit 11, pages 27–29
- Photocopiable Unit 11, Resource 1: Animal facts, page 88
- Photocopiable Unit 11, Resource 2: Animal vocabulary, page 89

Additional resources

- Non-fiction books about whales and sea creatures – make other non-fiction books about animals available in the class library
- Film clip about humpback whales
- Dictionaries
- Pictures of imaginary animals

Introduction

Teaching overview

In this unit children learn to write an information text (fact file).

The unit focuses on the structure of an information text that includes technical vocabulary.

Introduce the concept

Show a short film clip of humpback whales and discuss any facts that are presented.

Discuss with the children that information texts contain subject-specific technical language. Discuss with

the children the meaning of 'technical vocabulary'. It means words that are special to a particular topic and are often used by experts. Give examples of technical language about humpback whales.

Ask children to look out for the tense of the verb. Information texts like fact files are usually written in the present tense.

Read the text on Pupil Book page 27 together. Help the children to locate and understand specific vocabulary, present tense verbs and facts (not opinion).

Pupil practice

Pupil Book pages 27–29

Get started

In this activity the children are introduced to information about humpback whales. They need to read the text and add the missing words.

Answers

1. Humpback whales are <u>mammals</u>, not fish. [1 mark]
2. Humpbacks have <u>two big nostrils (blowholes)</u> on the top of their heads. [1 mark]
3. Adult humpbacks can stay under water for <u>up to 45 minutes</u>. [1 mark]
4. They are called humpbacks because <u>they arch their backs when they dive.</u> [1 mark]
5. Humpbacks are very big but they still face dangers like <u>strong currents, storms, getting caught in fishing nets or being hit by boats.</u> [1 mark]

Try these

Children retrieve the facts from the text and consider the technical vocabulary.

Answers

1. They are called humpbacks because they arch their backs when they dive. [1 mark]
2. Each humpback has different white, grey and black patterns under its tail. [1 mark]
3. They can dive to a depth of 180 metres. [1 mark]
4. Breaching is when they leap out of the water. [1 mark]
5. Mammals: warm-blooded vertebrate animals that give birth to live young. Blowholes: the nostrils of a whale or dolphin on the top of its head. [2 marks]

Now try these

Answers

The children create a spider diagram for whales using the information in the text. They then decide on a new animal and create a spider diagram for it, using facts they know or can research. The children use their new spider diagrams to write a fact file for their chosen animal.

1. Accept diagrams that reflect the model.

2. Accept children's reasonable choice.

3. Children should use the model and add their own researched facts.

4. Accept complete sentences, punctuated correctly.

You may wish to use the activities and photocopiables in **Support** and **Embed** to give differentiated support with these activities.

Support, embed & challenge

Support

Unit 11 Resource 1: Animal facts provides a template of a spider diagram for those needing additional support to complete the tasks in **Now try these** activities 3 and 4. Children choose their animal and add the facts in the circles. When completed, ask them to write four sentences about their animal using the facts in the diagram.

Embed

Before the children carry out the **Now try these** activities, ask them to use Unit 11 Resource 2: Animal vocabulary to capture the technical vocabulary about whales used in the text. Once the children have carried out planning activities in **Now try these** (activities 2 and 3) provide them with a fresh copy of the photocopiable and challenge them to write down at least two words about their new animal that they are going to use in their own text.

When the children are ready to write, encourage them to use their chosen technical vocabulary, the notes from their spider diagram, the present tense and facts, not opinions, to write their animal fact file.

Challenge

Ask the children to research facts about their chosen animal using books or the internet. They should add illustrations and a glossary for the technical vocabulary to their fact file.

Homework / Additional activities

Fact file

Show the children some pictures of imaginary animals and ask them to invent their own imaginary animal. They should draw their creature and then write their own fact file about it.

Unit 12: Explanation writing: Healthy eating

Overview

English curriculum objectives

- **Reading:** Year 2 pupils should be taught to develop understanding of what they read by being introduced to non-fiction books that are structured in different ways.
- **Writing:** Year 2 pupils should be taught to write for different purposes.

Building towards

Children will write a note from the school to parents explaining which foods should be in a packed lunch.

Treasure House resources

- Composition Skills Pupil Book 2, Unit 12, pages 30–32
- Photocopiable Unit 12, Resource 1: Healthy eating, page 90
- Photocopiable Unit 12, Resource 2: A healthy lunch, page 91

Additional resources

- Non-fiction books about healthy eating as well as other non-fiction books about the body and the digestive system
- Film clips about healthy eating and the need to have a balanced diet

Introduction

Teaching overview

In this unit children use their knowledge of healthy eating to write a note to parents (from the school) explaining what should and should not be in their child's lunch box.

The unit focuses on retrieving information and using this information in a new context.

Introduce the concept

Ask the children to share with one another what they like to eat.

Ask: 'Do you know what types of food are good for you?' 'Do you know what healthy eating means?'

Read the text on Pupil Book page 30 together. Discuss the information and ask the children to help you find the key words, such as digestion, growth, energy, and so on. Ask the children to locate the features of information text (facts, present tense, specific vocabulary, and so on). Make links to the Science curriculum and to what is in their lunch boxes or on the school dinner menu.

Pupil practice

Pupil Book pages 30–32

Get started

Ask the children to reread the text in pairs before completing the activity by locating the missing words in the text.

Answers

1. Food and drink have to be broken up into <u>very</u> <u>small</u> <u>pieces</u> for our bodies to use. [1 mark]
2. We call this <u>digestion</u>. [1 mark]
3. Foods like meat, fish, nuts, eggs, cheese and milk are important for <u>growth</u>. [1 mark]
4. Energy for playing and working comes from foods such as <u>potatoes, rice, pasta, bread and cereals.</u> [1 mark]
5. We also get energy from <u>fatty</u> and <u>oily</u> <u>foods</u> such as cooking oil, butter, nuts and seeds. [1 mark]

Try these

Children retrieve the facts from the text.

Answers

1. The text is about foods that are important for our health. [1 mark]
2. We need to eat a variety of food to make sure our bodies grow and stay healthy. [1 mark]
3. Foods like meat, fish, nuts, eggs cheese and milk are good for growth. [1 mark]
4. Potatoes, rice, pasta, bread and cereals, and fatty and oily foods are good for playing and working. [1 mark]

Now try these

The children write about their favourite foods then make notes about healthy food and create a diagram of a healthy lunch box. The children use the notes they have made to write a letter to parents (from the school) about what should be in their child's lunch box.

Answers

1. Accept complete sentences, punctuated correctly.

2. Make sure children have used the information provided.

3. You may need to remind children how to add labels.

4. Ensure children have the correct information and have punctuated the sentences correctly.

You may wish to use the activities and photocopiables in **Support** and **Embed** to give differentiated support with these activities.

Support, embed & challenge

Support

Before the children carry out the activities in **Now try these**, ask them to complete Unit 12 Resource 1: Healthy eating which asks them to consider which foods are part of a balanced diet and which are not. Once the children have completed their chart, ask them to carry out **Now try these** activities 1, 2 and 3. Before the children move on to write their note, discuss in a group what the children think it should say, verbally rehearsing sentences and helping the children to retrieve sentences from their planning activities (**Now try these** activities 2 and 3). Model how to write 'Dear parents' and how to write the head teacher's name at the bottom. (As the children are just writing a note, there is no need for an address or a date.)

Embed

Ask the children to use Unit 12 Resource 2: School dinners to create a labelled diagram of a healthy lunch box for **Now try these** activity 3. When the children have completed the planning activities and are ready to write their note, discuss the style and format needed for the note (perhaps sharing some simple notes sent home recently) and rehearse some sentences together before the children write.

Challenge

Ask the children to write to their head teacher putting forward the case to become a Healthy Eating school.

Homework / Additional activities

Healthy eating

Ask the children to discuss with their families the meals they have at home. They should then write a menu for a healthy family meal.

Unit 13: Stories set long ago

Overview

English curriculum objectives

- **Reading:** Year 2 pupils should be taught to develop understanding by becoming increasingly familiar with and retelling a wider range of stories, fairy stories and traditional tales.
- **Writing:** Year 2 pupils should be taught to develop positive attitudes towards and stamina for writing by writing narratives about personal experiences and those of others (real and fictional).

Building towards

Children will continue the narrative of a story set long ago.

Treasure House resources

- Composition Skills Pupil Book 2, Unit 13, pages 33–35
- Photocopiable Unit 13, Resource 1: Gruel for dinner, page 92
- Photocopiable Unit 13, Resource 2: What happened to Oliver? page 93

Additional resources

- Pictures of a 19th century workhouse
- Information books and websites about daily life in the early 19th century

Introduction

Teaching overview

In this unit children learn to write the ending of a story based long ago.

The unit provides opportunities to discuss stories set in the past and for children to continue a narrative.

Introduce the concept

Ask: 'How would go about writing a story set long ago?' Discuss how such a story is very different from a personal story and how they would need to do some research into the facts before they started writing.

Next ask: 'What do you know about everyday life 200 years ago?'

Discuss with the children what a workhouse was, and who would have gone there and why.

Read the opening of 'Oliver Twist' on Pupil Book page 33. Ask the children to locate the vocabulary that creates the historical setting. Discuss the use of the past tense and clarify the main characters and events.

Pupil practice

Pupil Book pages 33–35

Get started

Children add the missing words from the given text to the spaces in the sentences.

Answers

1. Nearly 200 years ago, a baby was born. His name was <u>Oliver</u> <u>Twist</u>. [1 mark]
2. He was born in a <u>workhouse</u>. [1 mark]
3. Oliver's workhouse was run by a man called <u>Mr</u> <u>Bumble</u>. [1 mark]
4. Gruel was a sort of <u>watery</u> <u>porridge</u>. [1 mark]
5. They made up their minds to ask for <u>more</u> <u>gruel</u>. [1 mark]

Try these

Children answer the questions to understand why Oliver asked for more and why Mr Bumble was so angry with him.

Answers

1. Because they were very poor [1 mark]
2. They worked hard making things like sacks or clothes. [1 mark]
3. Gruel – a watery porridge [1 mark]
4. Gruel did not fill him up and he was very hungry. [1 mark]

Now try these

Children engage with the text (activities 1, 2 and 3) by writing speech bubbles for the illustrations, showing what the characters are saying. They write sentences to continue the story, telling their version of what happened to Oliver after he asked for more.

You may wish to use the activities and photocopiables in **Support** and **Embed** to give differentiated support with these activities.

Support, embed & challenge

Support

Unit 13 Resource 1: Gruel for dinner provides speech bubbles for the children to use for **Now try these** activities 1, 2 and 3. Organise for the children to role-play the events of the extract in groups, possibly recording the drama, prior to writing the speech bubbles.

Embed

Ask the children to draw a storyboard using their ideas for how the story continues. Unit 13 Resource 2: What happened to Oliver? provides a simple template for this activity. Remind the children that their story should remain in the historical setting.

Challenge

Ask the children to write the prequel to the story. How did Oliver come to be in the workhouse? Children will need to research facts about this prior to writing.

Homework / Additional activities

Story from long ago

Ask the children to write another story set long ago. It could link with a topic they are studying at school.

Unit 14: Instructions

Overview

English curriculum objectives

- **Reading:** Year 2 pupils should be taught to develop understanding of what they read by being introduced to non-fiction books that are structured in different ways.
- **Writing:** Year 2 pupils should be taught to write for different purposes.

Building towards

Children will write a set of instructions for making a fruit salad, showing understanding of the text features.

Treasure House resources

- Composition Skills Pupil Book 2, Unit 14, pages 36–37
- Photocopiable Unit 14, Resource 1: Fruit salad, page 94
- Photocopiable Unit 14, Resource 2: Game instructions, page 95

Additional resources

- Instructions for games and recipes (for example, recipe cards). You could ask children to bring in instructions from home.

Introduction

Teaching overview

In this unit children learn to write a set of instructions.

The unit focuses on understanding the features of an instruction text, including the use of imperative (command) verbs.

Introduce the concept

Show a set of instructions and explain how they should be followed. Discuss what makes this easier (for example, numbering) and where else children have seen numbered instructions.

Explore the idea that a set of instructions is a non-fiction text that explains to the reader how to do something and how there are many different kinds of instructions, such as directions, recipes or how to play a game.

Discuss how instructions usually use imperative (command) verbs: because instructions tell the reader what to do, they always use lots of imperative (command) verbs like 'walk', 'mix' or 'throw'.

Ask: 'Have you followed a recipe before?', 'What were you making?' Discuss what aspects of the recipe made cooking or baking the dish easier.

Read the text together. Ask volunteers to find the features of an instruction text, for example, what you need, numbered points and command verbs. Point out the step-by-step approach – the order is important in a set of instructions. Ask: What would make the instructions easier to follow? (Illustrations.)

Pupil practice

Pupil Book pages 36–37

Get started

The children write sentences about their prior experience with instructions.

Accept answers that show understanding of the need for correct sequencing and a step-by-step approach.

Try these

Children consider the correct sequence of instructions as well as the appropriate tense and form of the verb (imperative).

Answers

1. pick up, put, staple, fold, press, fold, follow, stop, check, carry on, glue, press, cut   [1 mark]
2. It is important to write instructions in order so that a task will be completed successfully. [1 mark]

3. Accept instructions with time words (adverbials) that are appropriate.   [1 mark]

Now try these

Children write a set of instructions for making a fruit salad.

Answers

1. Check that children have included 'Things you will need'.
2. Check for imperative (command) verbs and numbering of instructions.
3. Accept flowcharts that show the correct sequence of tasks.
4. Check for evidence of proofreading.

You may wish to use the activities and photocopiables in **Support** and **Embed** to give differentiated support with these activities.

Support, embed & challenge

Support

Unit 14 Resource 1: Fruit salad provides a template for those needing additional support to write the set of instructions for making a fruit salad (**Now try these**).

Embed

Once the children have completed the activities in the Pupil Book (including writing a set of instructions for making a fruit salad), ask them to choose a game they know well and write a set of instructions to give to a friend telling them clearly what things they need and what they have to do to play and win the game. Unit 14 Resource 2: Game instructions provides a simple template for this activity.

Challenge

Once the children have completed the additional task (see **Embed**), ask them to swap instructions with a partner and try to use their partner's instructions to play a game.

Homework / Additional activities

How to get to ...

Ask the children to write a set of directions for walking from their house to their friend's house or to school. They could record it in the manner of a satnav voice.

Review unit 2

These tasks provide the children with the opportunity to apply and demonstrate the skills they have learned. Explain to the children that they now have an opportunity to show their skills independently.

A. Explanation texts

Read the task through with the children and make sure they have understood what to do. You may wish to give Review unit 2 Resource 1: Life cycle of a butterfly, page 96 to children to use as a template.

Look for evidence of children's developing understanding of and writing of explanation texts. Significant features to look out for include:

- the use of flowcharts or cyclical diagrams to show a process in chronological order
- the present tense
- technical language
- possible diagrams or illustrations.

B. Writing poems

Read the task through with the children and make sure they have understood what to do. You may wish to give Review unit 2 Resource 2: Arriving at school, page 97 to children to use as a template.

Look for evidence of children's developing understanding of and writing of poetry. Significant features to look out for include:

- choice of correct rhyming pattern
- choice of appropriate rhyming word
- appropriate subject matter.

C. Planning longer stories

Read the task through with the children and make sure they have understood what to do. You may wish to give Review unit 2 Resource 3: The old house and the treasure, page 98 to children to use as a template.

Look for evidence of children's developing understanding of planning a story. Significant features to look for include planning for:

- setting
- character
- plot – beginning, middle and end.

Unit 15: Poetry: Animal rhymes

Overview

English curriculum objectives

- **Reading:** Year 2 pupils should be taught to listen to, discuss and express views about a wide range of contemporary and classic poetry.
- **Writing:** Year 2 pupils should be taught to develop positive attitudes towards and stamina for writing by writing poetry.

Building towards

Children will complete a rhyming poem about the life cycle of a frog and go on to write a rhyming poem about an animal or insect of their choice.

Treasure House resources

- Composition Skills Pupil Book 2, Unit 15, pages 40–42
- Photocopiable Unit 15, Resource 1: Frog poem, page 99
- Photocopiable Unit 15, Resource 2: Three verses, page 100

Additional resources

- Non-fiction books about animals and insects, especially about the life cycles of frogs and butterflies
- A film clip of a caterpillar spinning a cocoon and then emerging as a butterfly
- Dictionaries

Introduction

Teaching overview

In this unit children learn to write a rhyming poem.

The unit focuses on the structure of a rhyming poem with links to the Science curriculum.

Introduce the concept

Show a short film clip of a caterpillar spinning a cocoon and then emerging as a butterfly. Discuss the life cycle and any technical vocabulary.

Remind children of rhyming words and discuss the fact that some poems rhyme. Discuss how poems can rhyme in different ways. Read 'Caterpillar' by Wendy Cope together. Point out that in this poem the rhyme structure (scheme) is *abcb*. Ask volunteers to locate the rhyming words.

Pupil practice

Pupil Book pages 40–42

Get started

In this activity the children are asked to summarise the poem by thinking about what has happened to the caterpillar.

Answers

1. He has turned into a butterfly.   [1 mark]

Try these

Children will need dictionaries in order to explain the technical vocabulary.

Answers

1. a) appetite: a desire for food   [1 mark]
   b) cocoon: a silky case spun by
      the caterpillar   [1 mark]
   c) emerged: came out   [1 mark]
   d) crimson: a deep red colour   [1 mark]
2. Accept sentences that use the words accurately.
3. The second and fourth lines rhyme.   [1 mark]
   Rhyming words:

   leaf / brief   by / butterfly

   tune / cocoon   sun / begun
                              [1 mark for each pair]
4. He didn't know that he was going to turn into a butterfly. He thought his life would end at that point.   [1 mark]
5. He has eaten lots of food.   [1 mark]

Now try these

The children research and draw the life cycle of a frog. They complete given stanzas 1 and 2 by providing a final rhyming word. Finally they write the last verse of the poem.

Answers

1. Accept drawings or flowcharts that show understanding of this life cycle.

2. belly

3. legs

4. Accept verses about froglets turning into frogs with some attempt at rhyming lines.

You may wish to use the activities and photocopiables in **Support** and **Embed** to give differentiated support with these activities.

Support, embed & challenge

Support

Unit 15 Resource 1: Frog poem provides the verses from **Now try these** plus a third stanza for children needing additional support. They add the rhyming words and draw pictures to accompany these.

Embed

Encourage the children to use the simple template on Unit 15 Resource 2: Three verses to write their own poem about a tadpole turning into a frog. Explain that they can use ideas – or the complete stanzas themselves – from the Pupil Book for stanzas 1 and 2 but they should write their own last stanza. Encourage them to attempt to follow the rhyme scheme.

Challenge

Ask the children to choose another subject to write a rhyming poem about. They should write three stanzas that have the same rhyme structure (*abcb*) as the poem 'Caterpillar' by Wendy Cope.

Homework / Additional activities

My rhyming poem

Ask the children to write a rhyming poem about a special time of year or a celebration.

Unit 16: Narrative

Overview

English curriculum objectives

- **Reading:** Year 2 pupils should be taught to develop understanding of what they read by becoming increasingly familiar with and retelling a wider range of stories, fairy stories and traditional tales.
- **Writing:** Year 2 pupils should be taught to develop positive attitudes towards and stamina for writing by writing narratives about personal experiences and those of others (real and fictional).

Building towards

Children will plan a story continuing from the extract, considering what happens to the main character.

Treasure House resources

- Composition Skills Pupil Book 2, Unit 16, pages 43–45
- Photocopiable Unit 16, Resource 1: Tig's story, page 101
- Photocopiable Unit 16, Resource 2: What happens to Tig? page 102

Additional resources

- A variety of familiar stories (stories that could serve as a prompt for dressing up for Book Day would be useful)
- A copy of *Stig of the Dump* by Clive King

Introduction

Teaching overview

In this unit children learn about narrative and how to continue a story.

This unit focuses on understanding the main character in a short narrative. It provides opportunities for children to discuss the character and why they act as they do, and consider how the narrative continues after the extract finishes.

Introduce the concept

Ask the children to share their stories of Book Day in school.

Ask: 'Have you ever dressed up as a character from a book?' 'Which one?' 'Which character did your

teacher dress up as?' 'Did the school do anything special?' 'What stories were read to you?'

Read the extract together, asking the children to tell you who the main characters are, what the setting is and which words are spoken by the characters. Ask: 'What clues are there in the story that Tig's costume might go wrong?' (Something went wrong last year.) Ask: 'What costume might Tig wear? How might this look? How might this be funny?' Show a copy of *Stig of the Dump* and ask: 'Has anyone read this book, *Stig of the Dump*?' If they have, ask the children to give a summary and tell the class why Stig acts as he does.

Pupil practice

Pupil Book pages 43–45

Get started

The children add the missing words from the story to the spaces in the sentences.

Answers

1. Tig had heard every word <u>Miss</u> <u>Simmons</u> had said. [1 mark]
2. Miss Simmons waved her hand at a display of <u>books</u> and posters. [1 mark]
3. 'You could be a <u>detective</u> or a hobbit or a <u>superhero</u>.' [2 marks]
4. All that day, Miss Simmons went on about <u>Book</u> <u>Day</u>. [1 mark]
5. At <u>playtime</u> everyone decided which characters they were going to be. [1 mark]

Try these

The children reread the text and answer the questions.

Answers

1. She wants them to come up with new ideas. [1 mark]
2. Take sensible answers such as 'a small trophy'. [1 mark]
3. This will be a personal answer based on the book the child is reading. [1 mark]
4. No. This is because his mother made a mistake with the costume last year. [1 mark]

Now try these

Children should use their prediction skills and imagination to continue the story by answering the questions. They should continue the story in written sentences or in pictures as a storyboard with captions.

You may wish to use the activities and photocopiables in **Support** and **Embed** to give differentiated support with these activities.

Support, embed & challenge

Support

Unit 16 Resource 1: Tig's story provides a structure for those needing additional support to tell their story. It provides a section for each question in **Now try these**. The children should to draw their plan and then to add a simple sentence next to it.

Embed

Ask the children to draw a story map using their ideas for how the story continues and ends using the prompts from **Now try these**. Unit 16 Resource 2: What happens to Tig? provides a template for the children to use. You might want to suggest that they use three boxes for the problem (Tig arrives in his costume, something goes wrong, it gets worse/people notice), two boxes for the solution (someone helps, or Tig changes the costume) and one box for the ending (perhaps Tig wins the prize).

Challenge

Ask the children to write another story based on the idea of Book Day.

Homework / Additional activities

Character description

Ask the children to write a description of the main character in the book they are reading at the moment. Include sentences about why the character acts as they do. They could think about the character Tig in the story and how he is embarrassed by his mother.

Unit 17: Non-chronological report

Overview

English curriculum objectives

- **Reading:** Year 2 pupils should be taught to develop understanding of what they read by being introduced to non-fiction books that are structured in different ways.
- **Writing:** Year 2 pupils should be taught to write for different purposes.

Building towards

Children will write a non-chronological report about an animal of their choice.

Treasure House resources

- Composition Skills Pupil Book 2, Unit 17, pages 46–48
- Photocopiable Unit 17, Resource 1: Animal key facts, page 103
- Photocopiable Unit 17, Resource 2: Animal report, page 104

Additional resources

- Non-fiction books and websites about animals and birds
- Film clips about animals and birds

Introduction

Teaching overview

In this unit children learn to write a non-chronological report. The unit focuses on the structure of a report.

Introduce the concept

Ask: 'Do you know any facts about keeping birds as pets, especially budgies?' 'What do you know about keeping other animals as pets?' 'What advice would you give to someone who wanted to do this?'

Discuss with children how they could write this advice down in a report and that, when we write reports like this, we organise our writing to make it easy for others to understand.

Introduce the report on Pupil Book page 46 and read it together. Ask the children to help you locate the features of a report, for example: key words, subheadings, present tense verbs.

Pupil practice

Pupil Book pages 46–48

Get started

In this activity the children decide which information is 'true' and which is 'false'.

Answers

1. true   [1 mark]
2. false   [1 mark]
3. false   [2 marks]
4. false   [1 mark]

Try these

Children retrieve the facts from the text and consider the different sections of the report.

Answers

1. Subheadings: Where they come from; Song; Handling your pet; Feeding   [1 mark]
2. Breaking it up into sections helps to organise the information.   [1 mark]

3. present tense   [1 mark]
4. Pictures and diagrams – they give important information too.   [1 mark]

Now try these

Children may use the photocopiables for support with this text type. Provide books, websites and film clips to help children choose and research their topic, then use the flow of activities here to create their report.

1. Children will plan and write a non-chronological report about an animal of their choice.
2. They use relevant subheadings to organise the facts.
3. Check that the present tense is used throughout.
4. Check for inclusion of diagrams or pictures.

You may wish to use the activities and photocopiables in **Support** and **Embed** to give differentiated support with these activities.

Support, embed & challenge

Support

Unit 17 Resource 1: Animal key facts provides a template to which children can add key facts about their chosen animal. They can add pictures to show the facts. This could form the basis of an oral report on their subject.

Embed

Ask the children to use the template provided (Unit 17 Resource 2: Animal report) as a framework for their non-chronological report. Explain that they can either use the subheadings provided in **Now try these** or choose their own subheadings. Remind them to check that they have used the features of a report in their writing.

Challenge

Encourage these children to use a greater range of subheadings and labelled diagrams or illustrations to present the information to the reader. They should open the report with an introduction.

Homework / Additional activities

Dinosaur report

Ask the children to write a non-chronological report about a dinosaur of their choice. They could record this as an oral report after it is written.

Unit 18: Traditional tales (2)

Overview

English curriculum objectives

- **Reading:** Year 2 pupils should be taught to develop understanding of what they read by becoming increasingly familiar with and retelling a wider range of stories, fairy stories and traditional tales.

- **Writing:** Year 2 pupils should be taught to develop positive attitudes towards and stamina for writing by writing narratives about personal experiences and those of others (real and fictional).

Building towards

Children will plan and complete a story based on the theme of greed.

Treasure House resources

- Composition Skills Pupil Book 2, Unit 18, pages 49–51
- Photocopiable Unit 18, Resource 1: Story flowchart, page 105
- Photocopiable Unit 18, Resource 2: Gold, page 106

Additional resources

- A selection of books and websites including traditional tales for children to browse and read

Introduction

Teaching overview

In this unit children learn about traditional tales and write their own middle and end to a story starter.

This unit focuses on some of the stock elements of a traditional tale (moral theme, a sudden visitor, asking for kindness).

Introduce the concept

Ask: 'Do you know of any stories where people argue a lot, especially over money?' Explain that this story is about two people who argue and who meet a mysterious little man.

Then ask: 'Have you read stories about hidden treasure?' Recount some to the group. Discuss if it is always lucky to discover treasure. Ask: 'Are there any stories where it is unlucky in the end to have found the treasure?'

Read the extract together. Ask: 'Do you think that Sandy and Bonny are going to end up rich by the end of the story? What else might happen?' Discuss different options. Explain that often in traditional tales greedy people do not usually end up rich! (Though kind people often do.) Ask: 'Do you think that the little man really needs somewhere to stay the night?' Discuss the traditional elements of sudden wealth, siblings, little people testing us, and so on.

Pupil practice

Pupil Book pages 49–51

Get started

The children add the missing words to the sentences using the text as reference.

Answers

1. Sandy and Bonny kept <u>sheep</u>. [1 mark]

2. The two of them were always <u>arguing</u>. [1 mark]

3. One evening, they were busy arguing when there was a <u>tap</u> <u>at</u> <u>the</u> <u>door</u>. [1 mark]

4. There on the doorstep stood a <u>little</u> <u>man</u>. [1 mark]

5. He wore a <u>green</u> <u>hat</u> and a <u>ragged</u> <u>green</u> <u>coat</u>. [2 marks]

Try these

Children answer the questions to give them an overview of the story, before suggesting the next events in the story, based on their understanding so far (and their understanding of traditional stories).

Answers

1. Because he took out two gold coins [1 mark]

2. greedy [1 mark]

3. gold coins/gold/treasure [1 mark]

4. Accept any appropriate answer. [1 mark]

Now try these

Children build on their ideas in **Try these** to write the middle and the ending of this traditional tale based on greed. Their sentences should begin where the text ends with Sandy spotting something gleaming.

You may wish to use the activities and photocopiables in **Support** and **Embed** to give differentiated support with these activities.

Support, embed & challenge

Support

Unit 18 Resource 1: Story flowchart provides structure in the form of a flowchart for the children to use to compose the end of their story using the process suggested in **Now try these**. Explain that each circle should cover one event.

Embed

Ask the children to use the storyboard provided (Unit 18 Resource 2: Gold) to plan the ending to the traditional tale (**Now try these**), adding accompanying sentences on the writing frame.

Challenge

Ask the children to write a new tale based on the theme of greed.

Homework / Additional activities

Greedy!

Ask the children to research other tales that contain a greedy character. They might think of fairy stories or other traditional tales they have read or seen on screen. They should then choose one of the characters, describe them and explain why they think they act as they do. Do they get what they deserved or not?

Unit 19: Myths

Overview

English curriculum objectives

- **Reading:** Y2 pupils should be taught to develop understanding of what they read by becoming increasingly familiar with and retelling a wider range of stories.
- **Writing:** Y2 pupils should be taught to develop positive attitudes towards and stamina for writing by writing narratives about personal experiences and those of others (real and fictional).

Building towards

Children will predict and write their own ending to a myth.

Treasure House resources

- Composition Skills Pupil Book 2, Unit 19, pages 52–54
- Photocopiable Unit 19, Resource 1: Daedalus and Icarus's escape, page 107
- Photocopiable Unit 19, Resource 2: What do Daedalus and Icarus do next? page 108

Additional resources

- Picture books of the Greek myths, in particular 'Theseus and the Minotaur' and 'Daedalus and Icarus'
- Film clips of these myths suitable for KS1

Introduction

Teaching overview

In this unit children learn how to continue a narrative based on a myth.

This unit provides opportunities to discuss stories or myths set in the past and for children to consider how the ending relates to the beginning. A myth is 'a well-known story that was made up in the past to explain natural events or to justify religious beliefs or social customs' (*Collins Dictionary*).

Introduce the concept

Ask: 'Have you heard of the word "myth"?' Explain what the word means and that the story today is based on a Greek myth.

Read the story on page 52 together. Help the children understand the story (including the back story of Theseus and the Minotaur). Read the tricky vocabulary together, explaining how the different names are pronounced. Discuss options for what might happen next – reminding them that this is the most difficult maze they can imagine but that it was designed by Daedalus himself.

After the children have written their story, tell them how the actual myth ends.

Pupil practice

Pupil Book pages 52–54

Get started

The children decide if the sentences are 'true' or 'false'.

Answers

1. true		[1 mark]
2. true		[1 mark]
3. false		[1 mark]
4. true		[1 mark]
5. false		[1 mark]

Try these

Children answer the questions to understand how the characters became trapped in the maze. This will help them as they plan the rest of the story.

Answers

1. the king		[1 mark]
2. Icarus		[1 mark]
3. He gave him string.		[1 mark]
4. They could not escape.		[1 mark]
5. Accept children's appropriate suggestions.		[1 mark]

Now try these

Children predict how Daedalus and Icarus will escape the maze, drawing a picture with speech bubbles and writing a caption to explain what happens. They then consider the ending. Their storyboards should help them to plan the sequence of events.

You may wish to use the activities and photocopiables in **Support** and **Embed** to give differentiated support with these activities.

Support, embed & challenge

Support

Unit 19 Resource 1: Daedalus and Icarus's escape provides a template for the children to use with **Now try these**. Ask them to use the large top box for their picture with speech bubbles of Icarus and Daedelus escaping the maze and the bottom two boxes for the end of the story. Once completed, the children could retell their story orally to an adult.

Embed

Ask the children to use Unit 19 Resource 2: What do Daedalus and Icarus do next? to capture their ideas from **Now try these**, writing accompanying sentences.

Challenge

Ask these children to research another Greek myth and retell it in their own words.

Homework / Additional activities

Local legends

Discuss with the children what a legend is and how this could be different from a myth (*Collins Dictionary*: 'A legend is a very old and popular story that may be true'). Ask the children to research a legend in their neighbourhood. They should write a few sentences summarising the legend.

Unit 20: Personal stories (2)

Overview

English curriculum objectives

- **Reading**: Year 2 pupils should be taught to develop understanding of what they read by becoming increasingly familiar with and retelling a wider range of stories, fairy stories and traditional tales.
- **Writing**: Year 2 pupils should be taught to develop positive attitudes towards and stamina for writing by writing narratives about personal experiences and those of others (real and fictional).

Building towards

Children will plan and write their own narrative.

Treasure House resources

- Composition Skills Pupil Book 2, Unit 20, pages 55–56
- Photocopiable Unit 20, Resource 1: My story mountain, page 109
- Photocopiable Unit 20, Resource 2: My storyboard, page 110

Introduction

Teaching overview

In this unit children learn about writing stories using their own experiences or those of others.

The unit focuses on the continuation of a story used in Unit 1 with the theme of helping one another. It provides opportunities to discuss these ideas and use them to plan and write such a story.

Introduce the concept

Ask: 'Has anyone ever helped someone or an animal that was in need?', 'Has somebody else helped you?'

Ask whether the children know of any other stories where animals or humans and animals help each other.

Reread the opening of the story on Pupil Book page 4 then read the continuation of the story on Pupil Book page 55. Ask the children to discuss in pairs why the animals are not scared of each other and how they might help each other. Ask: 'What can each of them still do?'

Pupil practice

Pupil Book pages 55–56

Get started

The children read the extract, copy out the statements and then decide if they are true or false.

Answers

1. false		[1 mark]
2. false		[1 mark]
3. true		[1 mark]
4. false		[1 mark]

Try these

Children answer the questions to show an understanding of the problem and begin to think about how the story might move on.

Answers

1. He had lost his smell. [1 mark]

2. He was old and weak. [1 mark]

3. Brown Bear was too tired and hungry to get up when Wilbur came near. [1 mark]

4. He is worried about how he will catch his food. [1 mark]

Now try these

Children should use their prediction skills, including knowledge of the story so far, to (1) draw (with speech bubbles) the next event in the story, (2) explain the problem each animal has and (3) draw how the animals help each other. Finally, (4) the children write their own new story about two different animals who help each other. Accept correctly demarcated sentences.

You may wish to use the activities and photocopiables in **Support** and **Embed** to give differentiated support with these activities.

Support, embed & challenge

Support

Unit 20 Resource 1: My story mountain provides structure for those needing additional support to plan their new story (**Now try these** 4). Tell the children to draw the three key events of their story in the three sections of the story mountain (moving from left to right).

Embed

Ask the children to use the storyboard template (Unit 20 Resource 2: My storyboard) to help them plan their story (for **Now try these** 4) and consider the sentences they will write.

Challenge

Ask these children to write their own story on the theme of helping friends, whether those friends are animals or humans.

Homework / Additional activities

Help

Ask the children to talk about a time when they helped someone or were helped by someone. They should write a few sentences about this time.

Review unit 3

These tasks provide the children with the opportunity to apply and demonstrate the skills they have learned. Explain to the children that they now have an opportunity to show their skills independently.

A. Non-chronological reports

Read the task through with the children and make sure they have understood what to do. You may wish to give Review unit 3 Resource 1: Bird report, page 111 to children to use as a template.

Look for evidence of children's developing understanding of and writing of explanation texts. Significant features to look out for include:

- present tense
- technical language
- headings and subheadings
- illustrations or diagrams.

B. Instructions

Read the task through with the children and make sure they have understood what to do. You may wish to give Review unit 3 Resource 2: How to make a sandwich, page 112 to children to use as a template.

Look for evidence of children's developing understanding of and writing of instruction texts. Significant features to look out for include:

- imperative (command) verbs
- sequential language
- logical order of instructions
- possible use of diagrams
- possible statement of purpose at beginning and statement at end
- numbered instructions
- diagrams to aid text.

C. Summarising a myth

Read the task through with them and make sure they have understood what to do. You may wish to give Review unit 3 Resource 3: Myth summary, page 113 to children to use as a template.

Look for evidence of children's developing understanding of myths and the ability to summarise them. Significant features to look for include:

- accurate summarising of the myth
- events in sequential order
- past tense
- sentences punctuated correctly.

What does Brown Bear do next?

What happens next to Brown Bear?

Draw your story in the boxes below.

My story is called _____ .
1	**2**
3	**4**

What happens next?

What happens next to Brown Bear? Plan your story by drawing pictures in the boxes below. Add sentences next to each box to tell the story.

My story is called _____.

My story map

Draw your story map showing how
the story continues and how it ends.
Draw pictures inside the boxes.

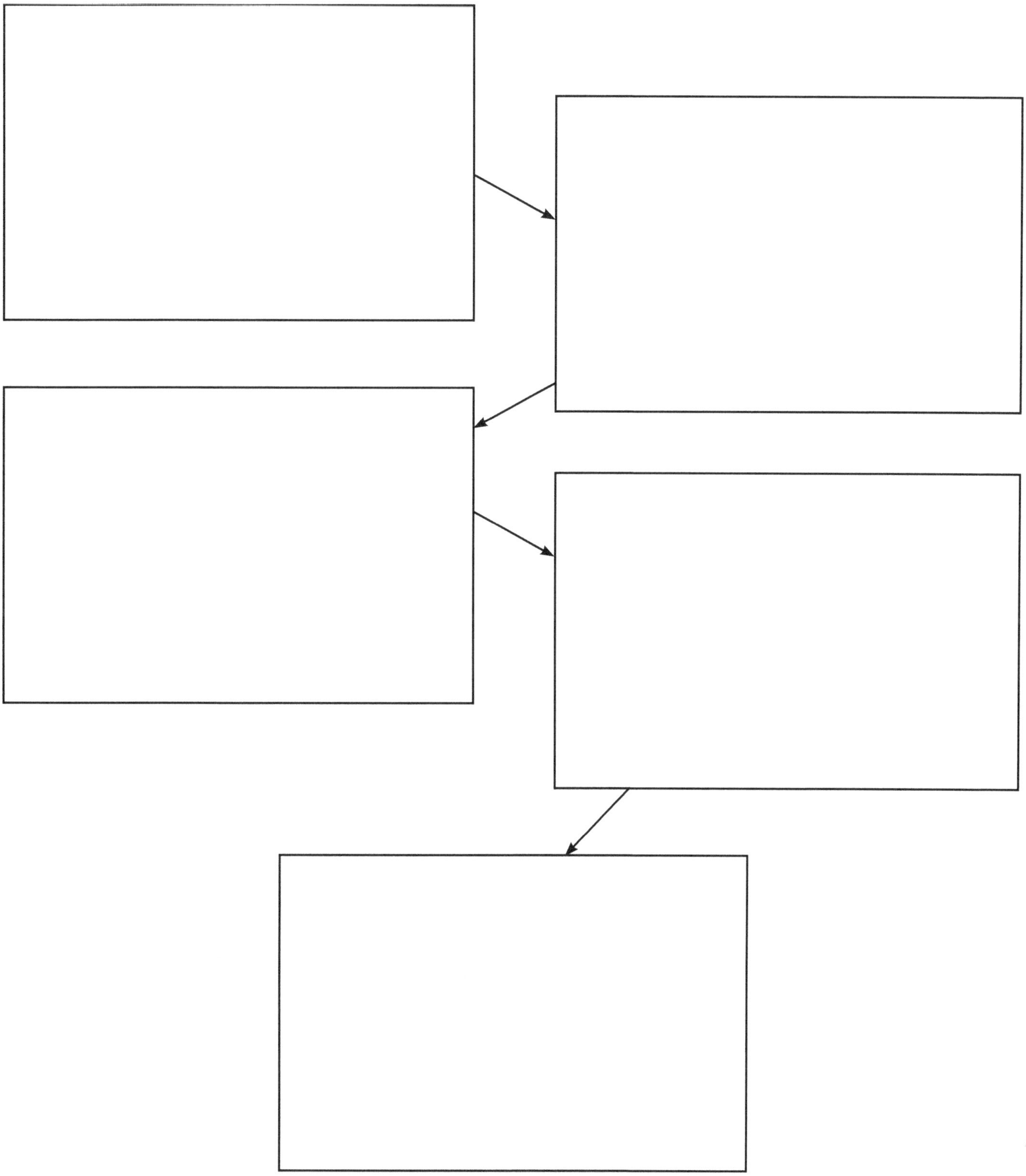

Fairy tale ending

How does your story about 'Puss in Boots' continue and end?
Plan your story by drawing pictures in the boxes below. Add sentences next to each box to tell the story.

© HarperCollins*Publishers* 2017

Hungry animals

Plan your story about an animal who takes some food.

Draw what happens under each sentence.

My story is called _____.

My animal is a _____	One day he takes _____
What happens next to him?	**How does my story end?**

Animal thieves

Plan your story about an animal taking food.

Draw pictures in the boxes below, then add sentences next to each box to tell the story.

My school

Complete the information text about your school.

Draw a picture of your school here.

My school is called _____.

It has _____ classes and _____children.

The head teacher is called_____.

I think my school is special because _____

_____.

What I like most about my school is_____

_____.

School report

Complete the information text about your school.

Draw a labelled illustration or map of your school here.
Where is my school?
How many children are there in it? How many classes? How many teachers?
Special things about my school – write in sentences. **1.**   **2.**   **3.**

Report template

Complete your report below. Add pictures.

My report is about _____.

Fact 1

Fact 2

Fact 3

My report

Complete the report below about your choice of subject. You may add labelled illustrations or diagrams.

My report is about _____.

Introduction

Section 1 – subheading

_____

Section 2 – subheading

_____

Section 3 – subheading

_____

How to …

Write a list of instructions for how
to _____ .

Draw a diagram in the box next to your instruction.

1	
2	
3	
4	
5	

Keep the classroom tidy

Write a list of instructions for how to keep your classroom tidy.

Include labelled diagrams. Check for imperative verbs.

1	
2	
3	
4	
5	

Riding a bicycle

Draw a picture of a bicycle.

Label the picture by choosing the words from below. Add the labels to your picture.

1. handlebars   **2.** wheels   **3.** chain

4. tyres   **5.** mudguards   **6.** pedals

Write a sentence under the picture to explain how to make the bicycle move.

How bicycles move

Draw a labelled diagram of a bicycle.

Add pictures into the flowchart to show how to make a bicycle move.

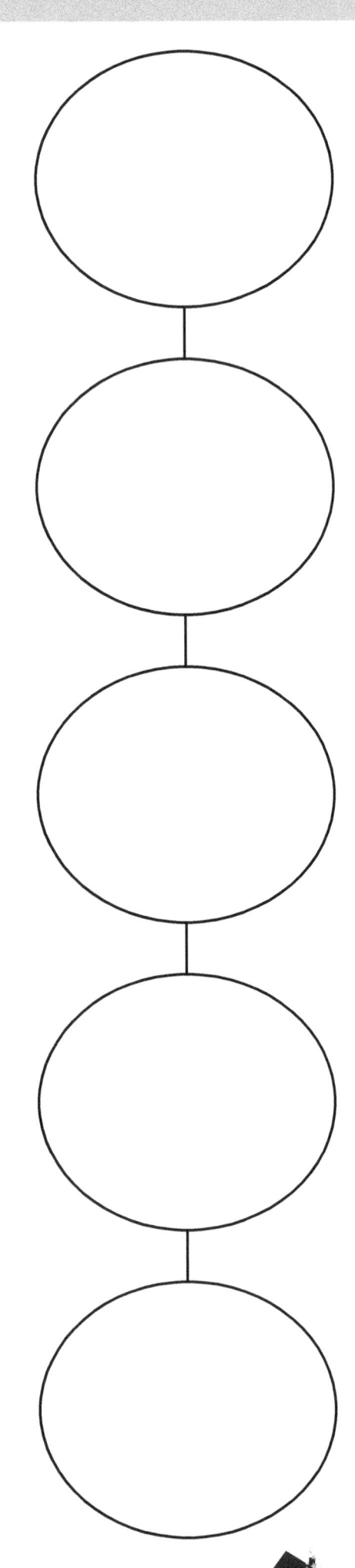

My town

Write a fact file or information text about the village or town where you live.

Title:

Opening sentence or sentences:

Information box 1	Information box 2

Information box 3	Information box 4

Diagrams or illustrations

Kim's birthday

It is Kim's birthday. She's seven years old and is hoping for a present from a special person. Write the story of her day.

Title: The surprise birthday present
Opening sentence or sentences:
Now write about what happened next. Was there a present or not?
How did the day end for your character?

How to play a game

Use this page to write the instructions for how to play a playground game. Remember to use command verbs. You may illustrate each step as you write it.

Title: Instructions for playing _____	
What you need:	
1	**2**
3	**4**
5	**6**

My toys

**Write some silly words about your toys below.
One has been done for you.**

Draw pictures of your toys in the boxes below.

My toy is Nee-noor-red.	
My toy _____.	
My toy _____.	
My toy _____.	

Toy poem

Write a silly poem about your toys. Start each line 'My toy ...' then write a silly description, for example, 'My toy is Nee-nor-red'.

My toy _____.

_____.

_____.

_____.

_____.

_____.

Animal poetry

Write a silly poem insulting an animal.
Start each line with 'Call', then write name of
your animal, then the description, for example,
'Call lion big paw'. Draw pictures to go with your poem on
the right.

My animal is a _____.

Call _____ _____

Call _____ _____

Call _____ _____

Call _____ _____

Call _____ _____

Call _____ _____

Call _____ _____

Insulting animals poem

Write a silly poem that insults a scary animal, such as a bear or a lion. Write and illustrate your poem in the space below.

My animal is a _____.

The Stone Cutter's story

Draw pictures to plan your ending of 'The Stone Cutter'.

My storyboard for how the story continues and ends	
The stone cutter wants to be the sun	The stone cutter sees something else he wants to be
The stone cutter sees something he wants to be	The stone cutter sees something else he wants to be
A last thing happens to the stone cutter	The stone cutter at the end

What happened next?

Draw your storyboard for the end of 'The Stone Cutter' here. Add sentences next to the pictures. Remember to keep the theme of your story in mind!

Animal facts

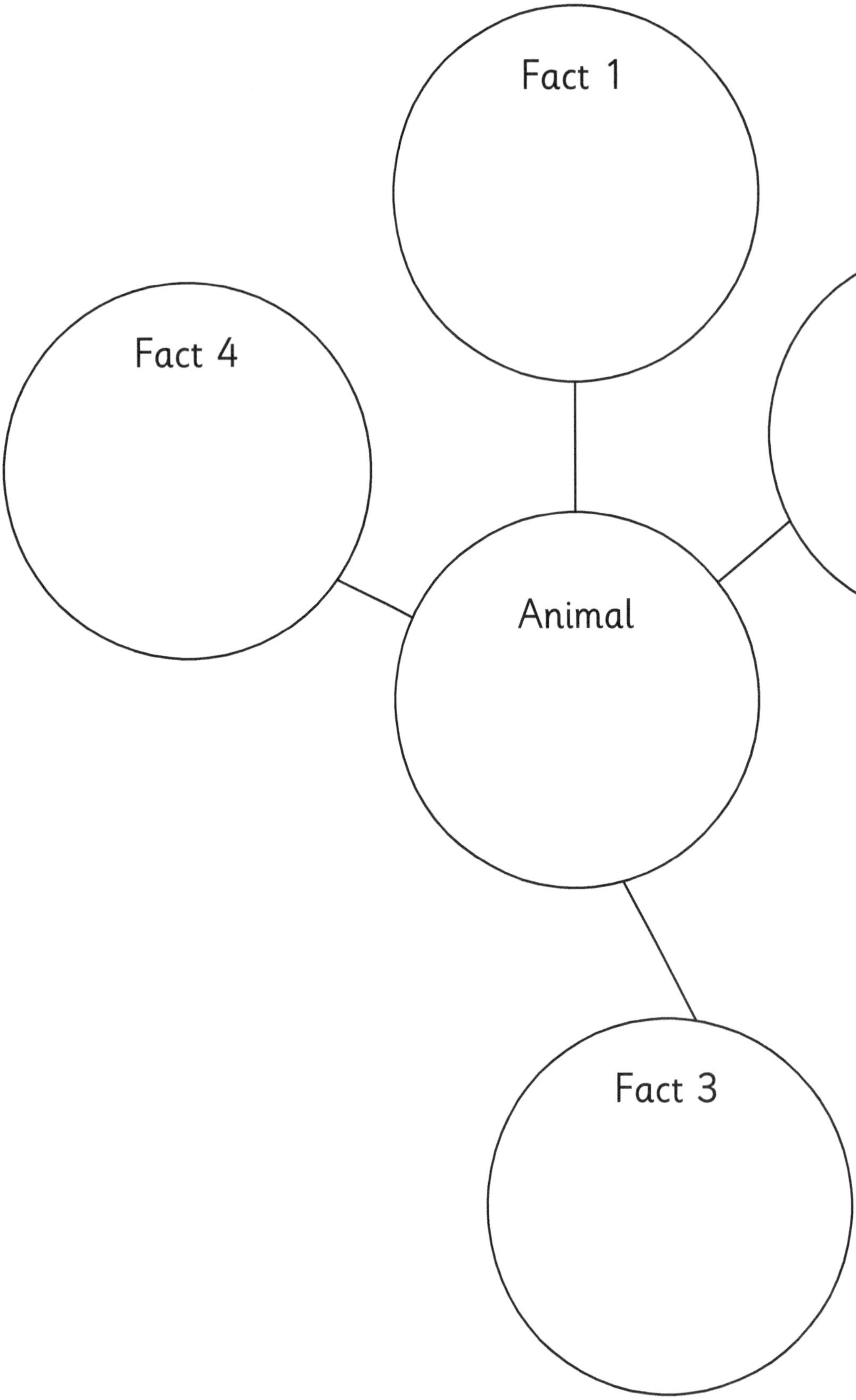

Fact 1

Fact 2

Fact 4

Animal

Fact 3

Animal vocabulary

Name of animal: _____

GLOSSARY	
Word	Definition

Healthy eating

Draw pictures in the boxes.

Foods that are good for me.	Foods that are not good for me.

A healthy lunch

Draw a picture of a balanced lunch box. Label the foods. Remember to include a healthy treat.

Draw three foods on top of the crosses that should not be in a lunch box.

Gruel for dinner

What do you think the boys said to each other when it was meal time and they were given gruel to eat? Write the words spoken by the boys in the speech bubbles.

What happened to Oliver?

Use the storyboard to plan what happens next to Oliver. Draw your ideas and write the sentences next to them.

Fruit salad

How to make a fruit salad.

Fill in the spaces with the ingredients you need to make a fruit salad.

Use the words below:

A small cup of orange juice

One apple

One banana

One pear

Add an ingredient of your own choice if you want.

Ingredients:

- _____
- _____
- _____
- _____

Now add a list of equipment. Use the words below:

A chopping board

A sharp knife

A large bowl

Three small bowls

Add a piece of equipment of your own choice if you want.

Equipment:

- _____
- _____
- _____
- _____

Finish the instructions by adding the correct verb to start the sentences.

Verbs: cut, divide, add, pour, stir, take

_____ three pieces of washed fruit.

_____ each piece into small pieces.

_____ the fruit to a large clean bowl.

_____ the orange juice into the bowl.

_____ the fruit salad until all the pieces are mixed.

_____ into three bowls.

Game instructions

Choose a game you know well and write a set of instructions to give to a friend that tell them what they need and what they have to do to play and win the game.

Fill in the spaces with the resources you need to play your game.	Resources • _____ • _____ • _____ • _____ • _____
Tell the reader clearly what they have to do in order to play and win the game. Remember to use a command verb to start each sentence.	

Life cycle of a butterfly

Draw a simple flowchart to show the different stages in the life of a butterfly. Write sentences to go with each part of the life cycle.

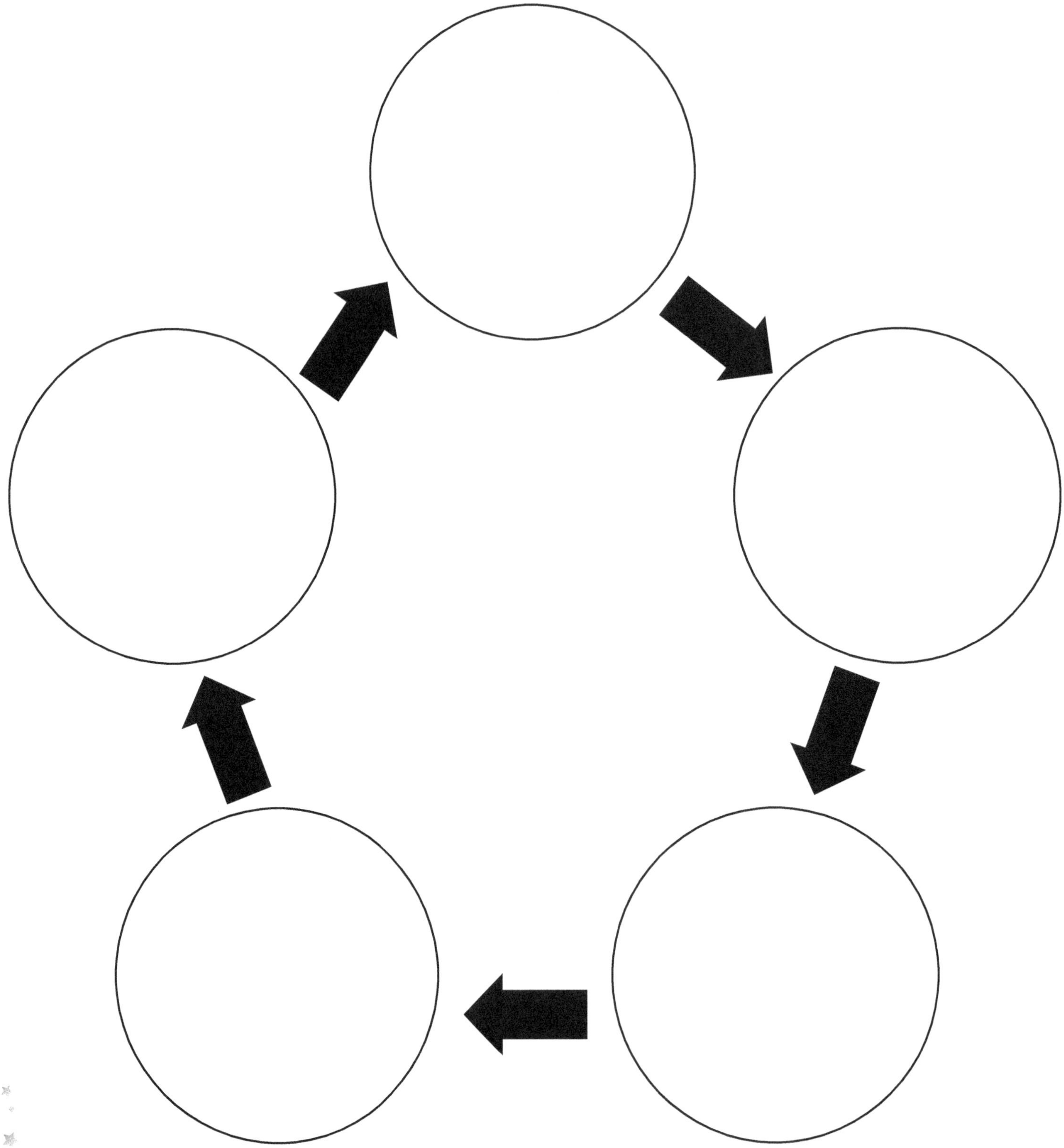

Arriving at school

Write a rhyming poem about children arriving at school in the morning that follows the pattern shown. The first one has been done for you.

In come the children two by two

They have many fun things to do!

In come the children three by three

_____

(Add your line here to rhyme with the line above.)

In come the children four by four

_____

(Add your line here to rhyme with the line above.)

In come the children five by five

_____

(Add your line here to rhyme with the line above.)

The old house and the treasure

Plan a story set in an old house. You need to choose two characters and it must include some treasure.
Who will be in your story? What will happen in your story?
Where and when will it happen? How will it end?

Title:	
1 Who are your characters?	**2** Where and when will it happen?
3 What will happen in your story?	**4** How will it end?

© HarperCollins*Publishers* 2017

Frog poem

Complete the poem and draw a picture for each verse.	Picture
Once a tiny tadpole Inside a blob of jelly Began to grow and grow and grow With the food inside its _____ .	
The tadpoles swam deep within the pond – They were no longer eggs. At first the back and then the front They found they had some _____ .	
They kicked their legs, they jumped about They landed on some logs. They croaked and croaked and croaked some more They now were jumping _____ !	

Three verses

Write your three verses here. Each verse should have four lines.

Draw pictures to go with your poem.

Verse 1	
Verse 2	
Verse 3	

Tig's story

Plan your continuation of Tig's story by drawing pictures in the boxes below. Add a simple sentence next to each picture to tell the story.

What costume does Tig wear? _____.	
The problem	_____ _____ _____ _____
The problem is sorted.	_____ _____ _____ _____
The end	_____ _____ _____ _____

What happens to Tig?

Use the storyboard to plan how Tig's story continues and ends. Draw your ideas and write sentences telling the story next to them.

	_____ _____
	_____ _____
	_____ _____
	_____ _____
	_____ _____
	_____ _____

Animal key facts

**Write key facts about your animal.
Draw pictures.**

My report is about _____	
What it looks like	
Where it lives	
What it eats	
Other facts	

Animal report

Complete the report below about your choice of animal. You may add labelled illustrations or diagrams.

My report is about _____

<u>Introduction</u>

<u>Section 1 – subheading</u>

<u>Section 2 – subheading</u>

<u>Section 3 – subheading</u>

<u>Section 4 – subheading</u>

Story flowchart

Plan the end of your story here. Draw what happens in the flowchart. Start with 1.

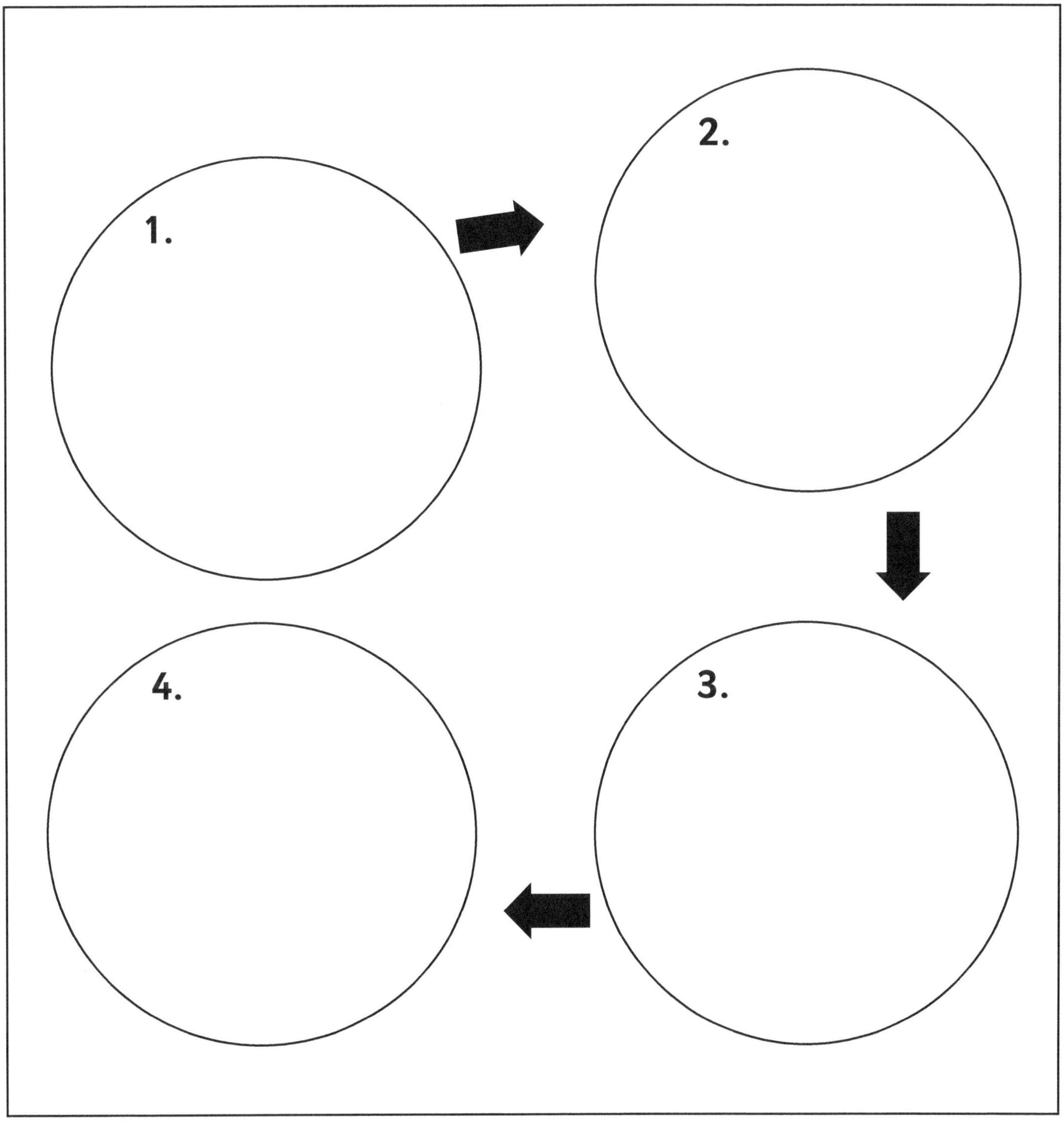

1.

2.

3.

4.

Gold

Plan the ending of your story in the boxes below.
Add sentences beside each box to tell the story.

Daedalus and Icarus's escape

My picture story: How Daedalus and Icarus escape the maze and what happens next.

1	
2	3

What do Daedalus and Icarus do next?

Draw pictures to show how the myth of 'Daedalus and Icarus' continues and ends. Write sentences about what is happening in the boxes next to the pictures.

© HarperCollins*Publishers* 2017

My story mountain

Plan your story on the story mountain. Add pictures to show what happens in your story.

My story is called _____.

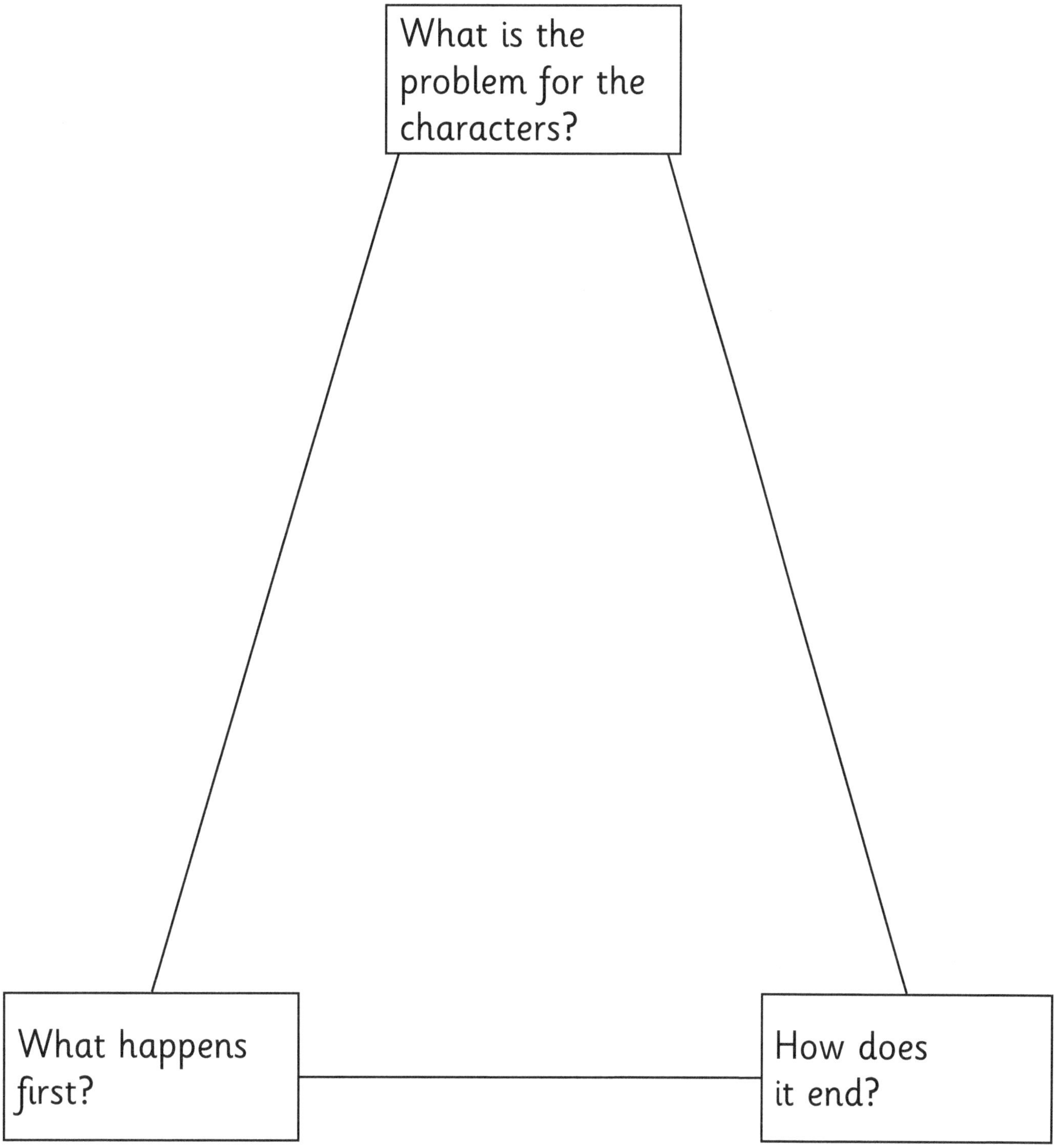

What is the
problem for the
characters?

What happens
first?

How does
it end?

My storyboard

Use the storyboard to plan and write your story.
Draw your ideas and write the sentences next to
them.

Bird report

Write a report about a bird of your choice. Research information and then decide how to present the information.

Name of bird:

How to make a sandwich

Write a set of instructions for making a sandwich of your choice.

Name of sandwich:
What you need for the sandwich:
How to make the sandwich:

Myth summary

Research a Greek myth of your choice. Summarise it in pictures as in a story map and add sentences under each picture to explain what is happening.

Title of myth:	
1	2
3	4
5	6